QUILTER'S Quick-Reference Guide

Your Essential Tabletop Companion

Measurement Cheat Sheet, Needle & Thread Tips, Quilt Sizes, Magic Cutting Numbers, Curved Piecing, Y-Seams, Binding & More!

C&T PUBLISHING
Another Maker Inspired!

Publisher: Amy Barrett-Daffin

Creative Director: Gailen Runge

Senior Editor: Roxane Cerda

Editors: Liz Aneloski, Betsy La Honta, Lynn Koolish, Gailen Runge

Technical Editors: Carolyn Aune, Helen Frost, Cynthia Hilton, Joyce Lytle, Nan Powell, Debbie Rodgers, Teresa Stroin

Cover/Book Designer: April Mostek

Production Coordinator: Zinnia Heinzmann

Illustrators: Jenny Davis, Mary E. Flynn, Debbie Rodgers

Photography Coordinator: Rachel Ackley

Cover photo by C&T Publishing, Inc.

Background photo, page 40: Kostikova Natalia/Shutterstock.com

Published by C&T Publishing, Inc., P.O. Box 1456, Lafayette, CA 94549

Printed in China

10 9 8 7 6 5 4 3 2

CONTENTS

4 Yardage

4 Yards to Inches
4 Fractions to Decimals

5 Needle & Thread

5 Stitch Tension
5 Sewing Machine Stitch Length Settings
6 Thread Weight
7 Needle Types
8 Needle Size Based on Fabric Weight
8 Uses for Various Needle Types
9 Needle/Thread Recommendations

10 Quilt Sizes

10 Bed, Comforter, Coverlet, and Bedspread Measurements
11 Customizing Your Quilt Size

12 Precuts

12 Standard Precut Sizes and Names
13 Cut Fat Quarters Into...
14 Cutting from 10″ × 10″ Squares
14 Cutting from 5″ × 5″ Squares

15 Cutting

15 Cutting Squares from Yardage
16 Cutting Numbers for Various Shapes

19 Piecing

19 Half-Square Triangle Units—Method 1: Sew and Slice, Two at a Time
20 Half-Square Triangle Units—Method 2: Eight From a Square
21 Half-Square Triangle Units—Method 3: Sheeting Triangles
22 Cutting Numbers for Stitch-And-Flip Flying Geese
23 Cutting Numbers for Four-at-a-Time Flying Geese
24 Cutting Numbers For Square-in-a-Square Block
25 Half-Rectangle Triangles
27 Corner Alignment for Piecing Shapes
27 Sewing Squares to Squares
28 Y-Seam Construction
29 Curved-Seam Construction

30 Borders & Backing

30 Mitered Border Corner Construction
31 Yardage for Quilt Backing

33 Binding

33 Cut/Finished Binding Widths
34 Yardage for Straight-Grain Binding
35 Faux Flange Binding
36 Cutting Bias Strips
36 Size of the Square Needed for Bias Strips
37 Mitered Double-Fold Binding Corner Construction
38 Seaming Double-Fold Binding Ends—Method 1
39 Seaming Double-Fold Binding Ends—Method 2
40 Seaming Double-Fold Binding Ends—Method 3
40 Three Options for Finishing Your Binding

Bonus Blocks!

To make the Quilter's Quick-Reference Guide as user-friendly as possible we've printed the reference information ONLY on the front sides of the pages, making it easy to flip to the information you need. So, as a fun bonus, we've added a quilt block to the back of each information page, each with a full color illustration, block construction and value diagrams, and cutting charts!

Practice your piecing skills on a few "challenge" blocks, use a single block on repeat to discover interesting secondary patterns (try Arkansas Crossroads or Flock) or create a sampler quilt with your favorite blocks! (Hint: 30 blocks made in the 12″ size can be arranged in a 5 × 6 grid to get a 60″ × 72″ quilt!)

How to Use the Block Charts

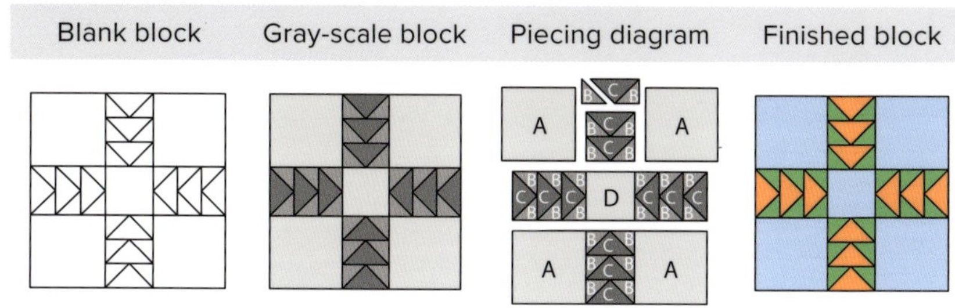

Which piece — How many to cut of each piece/fabric — How many you need of each piece/fabric — Finished block sizes

For	Cut	Need	4″	6″	8″	10″	12″
A	4 □	4 □	2	2¾	3½	4¼	5
B	12 □	24 ⧄	1⅜	1⅝	1⅞	2⅛	2⅜
C	3 □	12 ⊠	2¼	2¾	3¼	3¾	4¼
D	1 □	1 □	1½	2	2½	3	3½

CHART KEY

WOF = width of fabric

WOFQ = width of fat quarter (20″–22″)

Single dimension = □

Cut diagonally = ⧄

Cut diagonally, twice = ⊠

Width × length dimension = ▭

Questions? Here are the Answers.

4 How many inches are in that yardage?

5 Are my sewing machine settings right?

6 What do I consider when selecting my thread and needles?

8 What specific needle do I use?

10 What size should I make my quilt?

12 What are my pre-cut options?

13 How many pieces can I get from a fat quarter?

14 What pieces can I cut from a 10″ or 5″ precut square?

15 How can I cut fabric most efficiently?

16 What seam allowance should I add when I cut different shapes?

19 How can I save time and sew more than one half-square triangle unit at the same time?

22 What are the tricks to sewing together Flying Geese?

24 Can you save me time and do the math for a Square-in-a-Square block?

25 How do I sew half-rectangle triangles? Aren't they like HSTs?

27 How do I get my shapes to line up when sewing them together?

28 How do I sew Y-seams?

29 How do I sew curved seams… Should I be intimidated?

30 How do I miter my quilt borders?

31 How much backing fabric do I need?

33 How much yardage do I need for binding?

36 How do I cut one long bias strip?

37 How do I miter corners on my binding?

38 How do I join my binding ends?

BLOCK INDEX

4B

5B

6B

7B

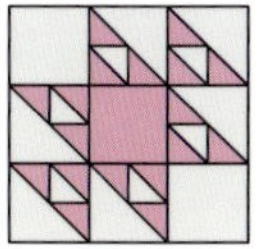
8B

9B

10B

11B

12B

13B

14B

15B

16B

17B

18B

19B

20B

21B

22B

23B

24B

25B

26B

27B

28B

29B

30B

31B

32B

33B

34B

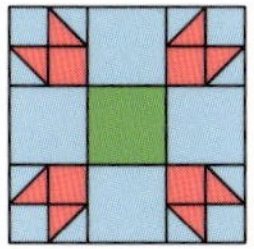
35B

36B

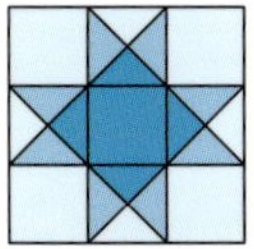
37B

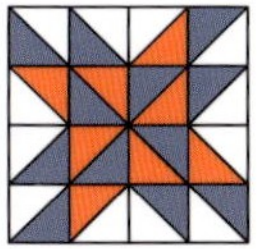
38B

39B

How many inches are in that yardage?

Yards to Inches

YARDS	INCHES	YARDS	INCHES
⅛	4½	1	36
¼	9	2	72
⅓	12	3	108
⅜	13½	4	144
½	18	5	180
⅝	22½	6	216
⅔	24	7	252
¾	27	8	288
⅞	31½	9	324
		10	360

Fractions to Decimals

Yardage, and many other quilting measurements, uses fractions. When working on calculations (multiplying shapes by the number of pieces needed, for example), it's often easier to work in decimals than in fractions. Here are the decimal equivalents to common quilt fractions.

FRACTIONS	DECIMALS	FRACTIONS	DECIMALS
⅛	0.125	⅝	0.625
¼	0.25	¾	0.75
⅜	0.375	⅞	0.875
½	0.5	1	1

BONUS BLOCK

Air Castle

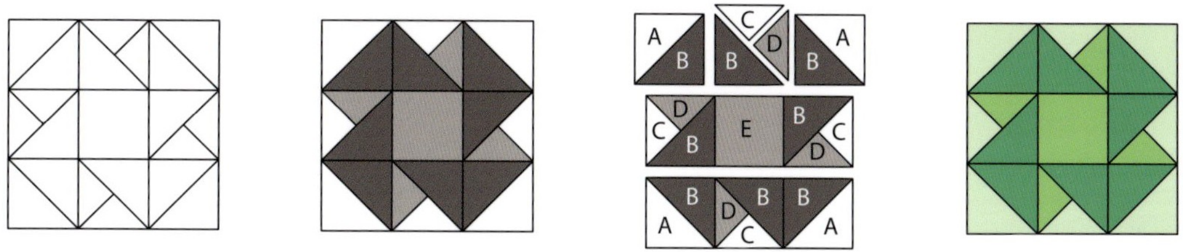

For	Cut	Need	3″	6″	9″	12″	15″
A	2 □	4 ⧄	1⅞	2⅞	3⅞	4⅞	5⅞
B	4 ■	8 ⧄	1⅞	2⅞	3⅞	4⅞	5⅞
C	1 □	4 ⊠	2¼	3¼	4¼	5¼	6¼
D	1 ■	4 ⊠	2¼	3¼	4¼	5¼	6¼
E	1 ■	1 ■	1½	2½	3½	4½	5½

Stitch Tension

Most stitching is done with a mid-range, balanced tension setting. The needle thread tension can be adjusted for different fabrics and stitch types. A high-tension setting gives tight stitches that are strong but more prone to breakage or puckering. A low-tension setting gives loose stitches that are useful for basting or gathering. The bobbin thread tension is generally not adjusted unless there is a problem with the stitching.

Balanced tension

Tighten your needle thread tension
(This shows low needle thread tension or high bobbin thread tension.)

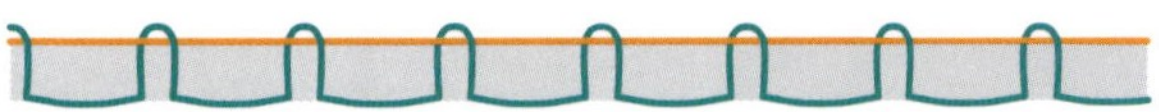

Loosen your needle thread tension
(This shows high needle thread tension or low bobbin thread tension.)

Sewing Machine Stitch Length Settings

MILLIMETERS	STITCHES PER INCH
0.5	50
1	25
1.5	16
2	12
2.5	10
3	8
3.5	7
4	6
4.5–5	5

BONUS BLOCK

Arizona

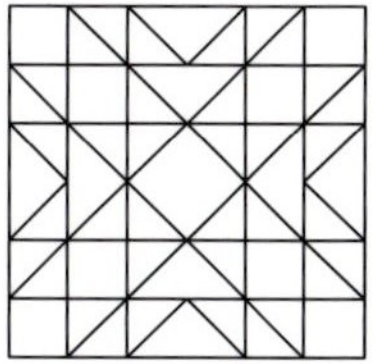

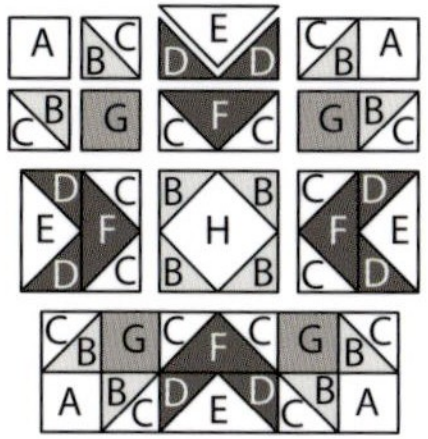

For	Cut	Need	3″	6″	9″	12″	15″
A	4 □	4 □	1	1½	2	2½	3
B	6 □	12 ⧄	1⅜	1⅞	2⅜	2⅞	3⅜
C	8 □	16 ⧄	1⅜	1⅞	2⅜	2⅞	3⅜
D	4 ■	8 ⧄	1⅜	1⅞	2⅜	2⅞	3⅜
E	1 □	4 ⊠	2¼	3¼	4¼	5¼	6¼
F	1 ■	4 ⊠	2¼	3¼	4¼	5¼	6¼
G	4 □	4 □	1	1½	2	2½	3
H	1 □	1 □	1¼	2	2⅝	3⅜	4

5B

Thread Weight

Standard measuring system: The thicker the thread, the lower the weight designation.

WEIGHT	FEATURES/APPLICATION
100	Very fine polyester or silk thread for nearly invisible stitching that sinks into and blends with the fabric.
70	Cotton or transparent thread used in bobbins and heirloom sewing.
60	Thin thread used in bobbins and for sewing thin fabrics.
50	Fine thread popular for quilting and topstitching.
40	Good balance of strength and delicate appearance. Standard weight for machine embroidery threads.
30	General-purpose sewing thread.
16–28	Thicker thread for upholstery, other heavyweight fabrics, and hand stitching.
10–12	Heavy-duty thread for outdoor use, attaching buttons, and craft sewing.

BONUS BLOCK

Arkansas Crossroads

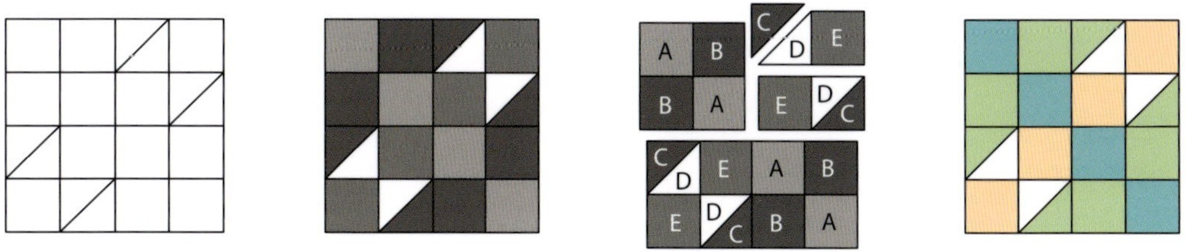

For	Cut	Need	4″	6″	8″	10	12″
A	4	4	1½	2	2½	3	3½
B	4	4	1½	2	2½	3	3½
C	2	4	1⅞	2⅜	2⅞	3⅜	3⅞
D	2	4	1⅞	2⅜	2⅞	3⅜	3⅞
E	4	4	1½	2	2½	3	3½

Needle Types

Needle sharpness, silhouette, and eye shape are optimized for different fabrics and applications. General home sewing needles are designated by the letter H. A second letter may be assigned to denote the purpose and/or specific fabric.

TYPE	FEATURES/PURPOSE
Universal (H)	Slightly rounded point suitable for most woven, and some knit, fabrics.
Ball-point (H)	Rounded point for sewing knit fabrics such as jersey and interlock.
Stretch (H-S)	Rounded point for sewing elastic and highly stretchy knits. Designed to prevent skipped stitches.
Sharp (H-M)	Also called a microtex. The slim point is ideal for precision piecing and topstitching on most woven fabrics, especially microfiber fabrics.
Embroidery (H-E)	For decorative stitching and machine embroidery. Designed to protect delicate threads during rapid back-and-forth stitching motion.
Quilting (H-Q)	Tapered point for piecing and quilting multiple layers.
Denim (H-J)	Reinforced and shaped for thick or tightly woven fabrics, such as denim and heavy canvas.
Leather (H-LL)	Cutting point for leather and nonwoven synthetics.

Specialty Needles

Designed for specific stitches and threads, these needles include hem-stitch, top-stitch, and metallic needles. Twin and triple needles create rows of parallel stitching.

BONUS BLOCK

Aztec Jewel

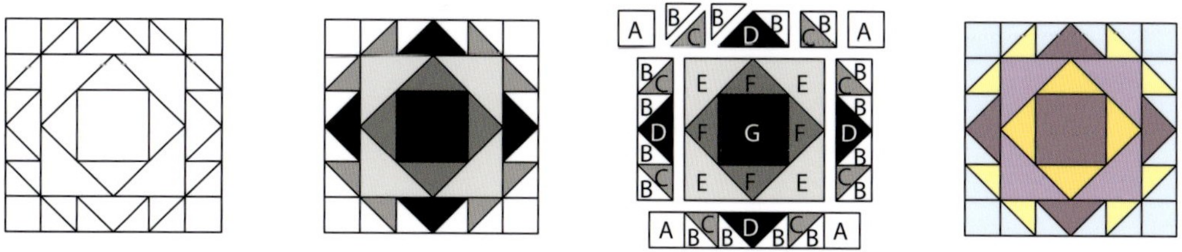

For	Cut	Need	3″	6″	9″	12″	15″
A	4	4	1	1½	2	2½	3
B	8	16	1⅜	1⅞	2⅜	2⅞	3⅜
C	4	8	1⅜	1⅞	2⅜	2⅞	3⅜
D	1	4	2¼	3¼	4¼	5¼	6¼
E	2	4	1⅞	2⅞	3⅞	4⅞	5⅞
F	1	4	2¼	3¼	4¼	5¼	6¼
G	1	1	1½	2½	3½	4½	5½

Needle Size Based on Fabric Weight

	LIGHTWEIGHT FABRICS			MEDIUM-WEIGHT FABRICS			HEAVYWEIGHT FABRICS		
EUROPEAN	60	65	70	75	80	90	100	110	120
U.S.	8	9	10	11	12	14	16	18	20

Uses for Various Needle Types

NEEDLE TYPE—TECHNIQUE	NEEDLE SIZE	FABRIC
H—piecing and quilting	80/12	Quilting-weight cottons
H-J Denim—piecing	75/11	
H-Q Quilting—quilting	80/12	
H-J Denim—piecing	80/12	Heavier cottons
H-Q Quilting—quilting	90/14	Flannels
H-M Sharp—piecing	70/10	Silks, satins, and delicate fabrics
H-M Sharp—piecing and machine embroidery	80/12, 90/14	Any fabric using metallic or heavy machine embroidery threads
H-E Embroidery—embroidery	75/11, 90/14	Any fabric using rayon threads

BONUS BLOCK

Cat's Cradle

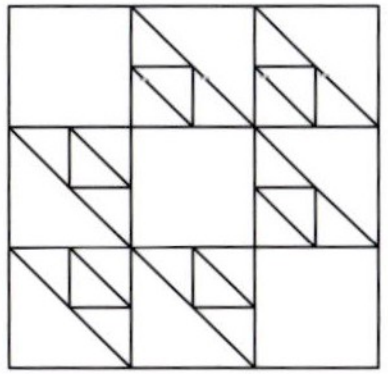

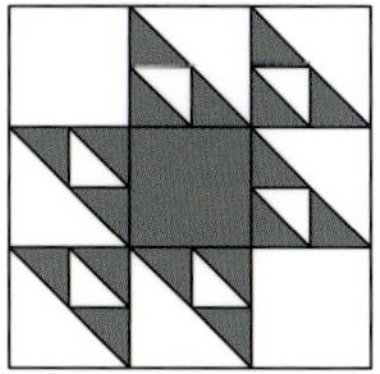

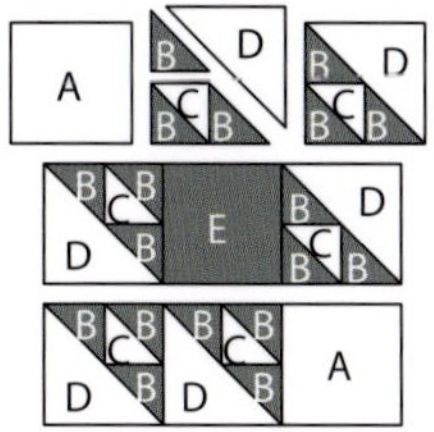

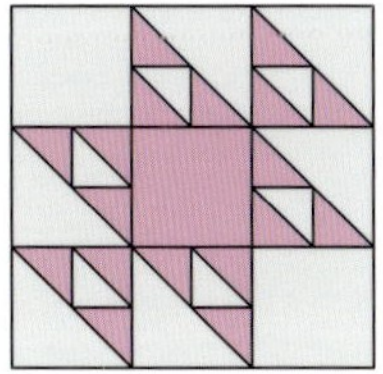

For	Cut	Need	3″	6″	9″	12″	15″
A	2 □	2 □	1½	2½	3½	4½	5½
B	9 ■	18 ◪	1⅜	1⅞	2⅜	2⅞	3⅜
C	3 □	6 ⧄	1⅜	1⅞	2⅜	2⅞	3⅜
D	3 □	6 ⧄	1⅞	2⅞	3⅞	4⅞	5⅞
E	1 ■	1 ■	1½	2½	3½	4½	5½

Needle/Thread Recommendations

THREAD	NEEDLE							
	60/8	65/9	70/10	75/11	80/12	90/14	100/16	110/18
Ultra fine 80	●	●						
Nylon monofilament	●	●	●	●	●			
Fine machine embroidery 60		●	●	●				
DMC machine embroidery thread 50		●	●	●				
Embroidery thread 30			●	●	●			
Mercerized cotton sewing thread 50				●	●			
Synthetic sewing thread (spun)				●	●			
Cotton-wrapped polyester						●		
Cotton 40						●	●	
Buttonhole (cordonnet)							●	●

BONUS BLOCK

Cross Variation

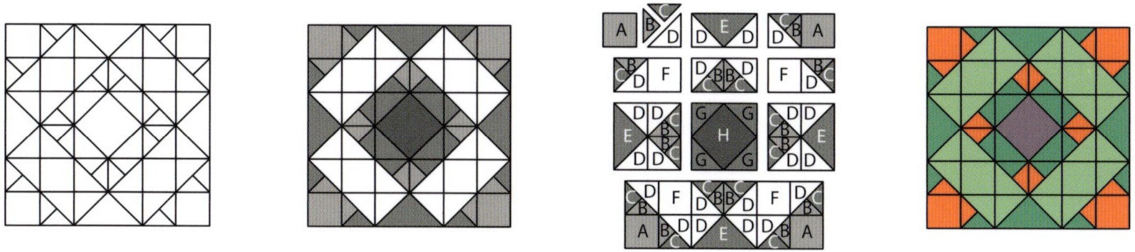

For	Cut	Need	6″	9″	12″	15″	18″
A	4 □	4 □	1½	2	2½	3	3½
B	4 □	16 ⊠	2¼	2¾	3¼	3¾	4¼
C	4 ■	16 ⊠	2¼	2¾	3¼	3¾	4¼
D	12 □	24 ◪	1⅞	2⅜	2⅞	3⅜	3⅞
E	1 ■	4 ⊠	3¼	4¼	5¼	6¼	7¼
F	4 □	4 □	1½	2	2½	3	3½
G	2 ■	4 ◪	1⅞	2⅜	2⅞	3⅜	3⅞
H	1 ■	1 ■	2	2⅝	3⅜	4	4¾

Bed, Comforter, Coverlet, and Bedspread Measurements

BED	MATTRESS SIZE (Inches)	COMFORTER (Inches)	COVERLET (Inches)	BEDSPREAD (Inches)
Crib	27 × 52			
Youth	32 × 66	56 × 78	64 × 92	74 × 97
Studio/cot	30 × 75	54 × 87	62 × 101	72 × 106
Twin	39 × 75	63 × 87	71 × 101	81 × 106
Twin, XL	39 × 80	63 × 92	71 × 106	81 × 111
Double/full	54 × 75	78 × 87	86 × 101	96 × 106
Queen	60 × 80	84 × 92	92 × 106	102 × 111
King	78 × 80	102 × 92	110 × 106	120 × 111
California king	72 × 84	96 × 96	104 × 110	114 × 115

Comforters cover the mattress but not the box spring and generally don't have a pillow tuck.

Coverlets cover the mattress and box spring and generally have a pillow tuck.

Bedspreads cover the bed to almost the floor and have a pillow tuck.

BONUS BLOCK

Darting Birds

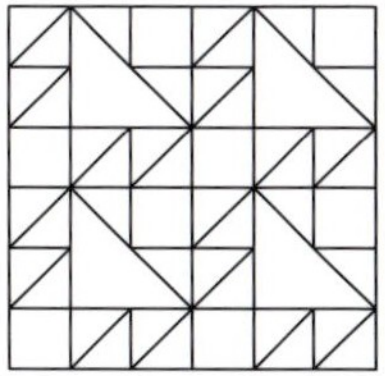
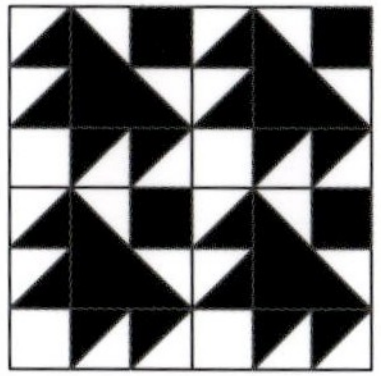
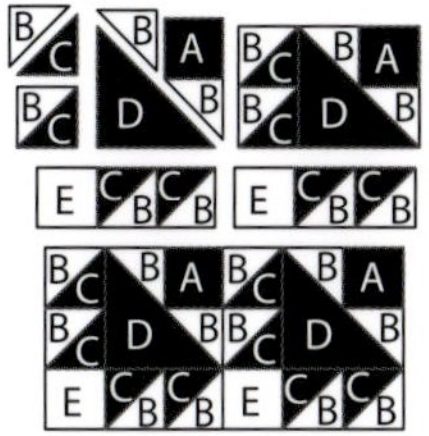

For	Cut	Need	3″	6″	9″	12″	15″
A	4 ■	4 ■	1	1½	2	2½	3
B	12 □	24 ⧄	1⅜	1⅞	2⅜	2⅞	3⅜
C	8 ■	16 ◩	1⅜	1⅞	2⅜	2⅞	3⅜
D	2 ■	4 ◩	1⅞	2⅞	3⅞	4⅞	5⅞
E	4 □	4 □	1	1½	2	2½	3

Customizing Your Quilt Size

Referring to the bed illustration and formulas, use your own bed measurements to determine the size quilt you need.

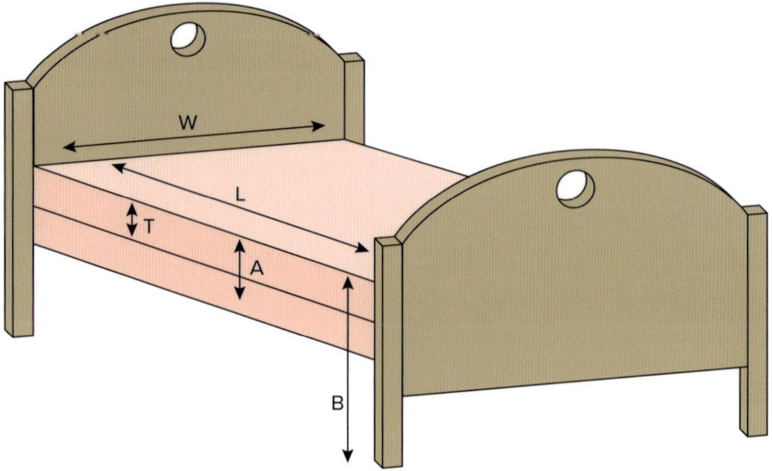

A = distance from top to dust ruffle

B = distance from top to floor

L = mattress length

W = mattress width

T = mattress thickness

PT = pillow tuck allowance (approximately 10″)

CR = contraction rate (quilt and batting shrinkage: 3%–5%)

QUILT TYPE	WIDTH	LENGTH
Blanket (4″ tuck allowance)	W + 2T + 8″ + CR	L + 1T + 4″ + CR
Comforter	W + 2T + CR	L + 1A + CR
Coverlet (tucked under pillow)	W + 2A + CR	L + 1A + PT + CR
Bedspread	W + 2B + CR	L + 1B + PT + CR

BONUS BLOCK

Flock

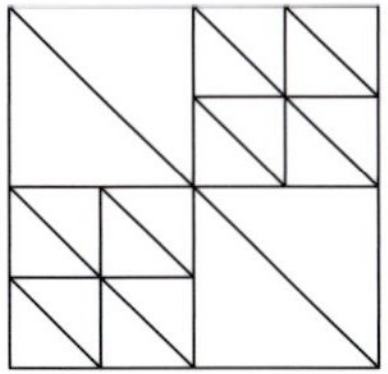

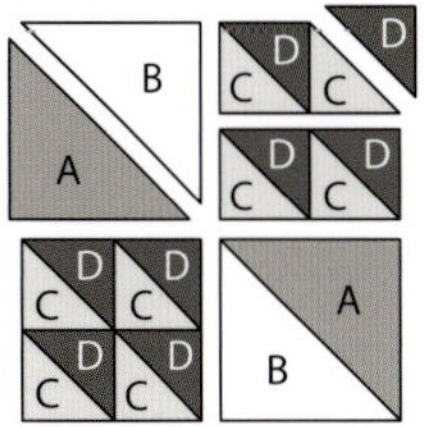

For	Cut	Need	4″	6″	8″	10″	12″
A	1	2	2⅞	3⅞	4⅞	5⅞	6⅞
B	1	2	2⅞	3⅞	4⅞	5⅞	6⅞
C	4	8	1⅞	2⅜	2⅞	3⅜	3⅞
D	4	8	1⅞	2⅜	2⅞	3⅜	3⅞

Standard Precut Sizes and Names

SIZE	NAME	NUMBER OF PIECES IN BUNDLE	APPROX YARDAGE INCLUDED
YARDAGE			
18″ × 21″–22″	Fat quarters	Varies	Varies
9″ × 21″–22″	Fat eighths	Varies	Varies
SQUARES			
10″ × 10″	Layer Cakes, Bali Crackers, Patty Cakes, Stackers, Stack Pack, Sundae, Ten Squares, Tiles, 10″ Stackers, Stacks, 10 Karat Gems, and more	40–42	2¾ yards
5″ × 5″	Charm Squares, Stamps, Chips, Stackers, Bali Snaps, Single Scoops, 5 Karat Gems, and more	40–42	½ yard
2½″ × 2½″	Candy, Mini Charm Squares	40–42	¼ yard
STRIPS			
2½″ × WOF	Jelly Rolls, Bali Pops, Design Rolls, Double Scoops, Pixie Strips, Rolie Polies, Roll Ups, Stone Strips, Strip Pack, Strip-pies, Roll Ups, 40 Karat Gems, and more	30–42	2¾ yards
1½″ × WOF	Honey Buns, Skinny Strips	40–41	1⅔ yards

BONUS BLOCK

House

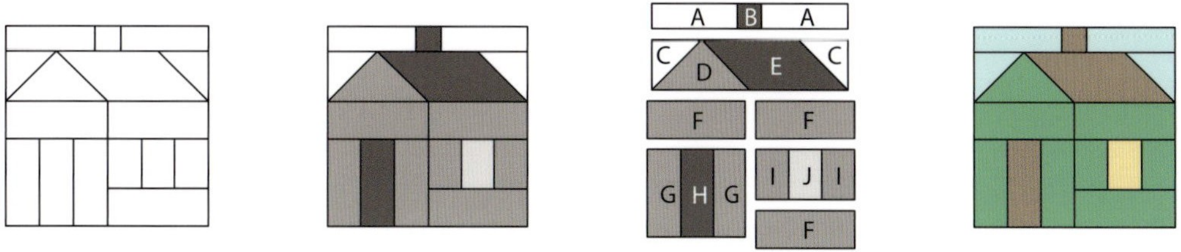

For	Cut	Need	4″	6″	8″	10″	12″
A	2	2	1 × 2¼	1¼ × 3⅛	1½ × 4	1¾ × 4⅞	2 × 5¾
B	1	1	1	1¼	1½	1¾	2
C	1	2	1⅞	2⅜	2⅞	3⅜	3⅞
D	1	1	3¼	4¼	5¼	6¼	7¼
E*	1	1	1½ × 4¼	2 × 5¾	2½ × 7¼	3 × 8¾	3½ × 10¼
F	3	3	1¼ × 2½	1⅝ × 3½	2 × 4½	2⅜ × 5½	2¾ × 6½
G	2	2	1⅛ × 2¼	1½ × 3⅛	1¾ × 4	2⅛ × 4⅞	2½ × 5¾
H	1	1	1¼ × 2¼	1½ × 3⅛	2 × 4	2¼ × 4⅞	2½ × 5¾
I	2	2	1⅛ × 1½	1½ × 2	1¾ × 2½	2⅛ × 3	2½ × 3½
J	1	1	1¼ × 1½	1½ × 2	2 × 2½	2¼ × 3	2½ × 3½

For E rectangle, place the 45° line of the rotary ruler on the edge of the fabric and trim as shown. Rotate the ruler and repeat if necessary.

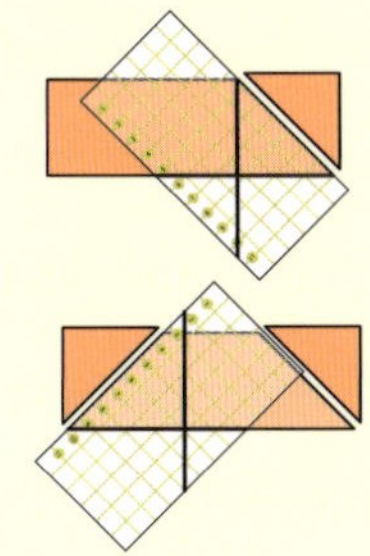

**Trim the corners of the E rectangle using the 45° line on a rotary ruler.*

How many pieces can I get from a fat quarter?

Cut Fat Quarters Into...

56 squares 2½″ × 2½″

42 squares 3″ × 3″

30 squares 3½″ × 3½″

20 squares 4″ × 4″

16 squares 4½″ × 4½″

12 squares 5″ × 5″

12 squares 5½″ × 5½″

9 squares 6″ × 6″

6 squares 6½″ × 6½″

6 squares 7″ × 7″

4 squares 7½″ × 7½″

4 squares 8″ × 8″

4 squares 8½″ × 8½″

2 squares 10″ × 10″

Efficient use of a fat quarter:

2 squares 10″ × 10″

4 squares 5″ × 5″

1 strip 2½″ × 22″

1 strip 2″ × 15″

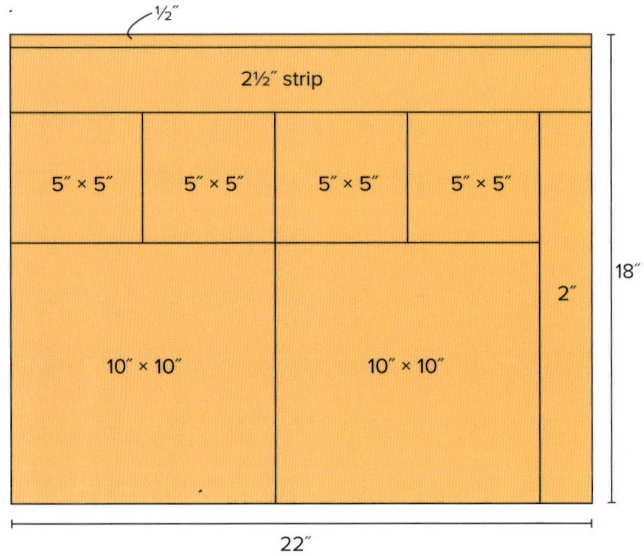

BONUS BLOCK

Jacob's Ladder B

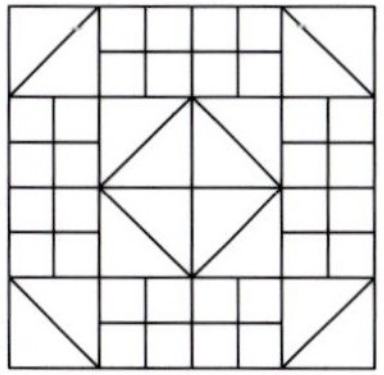

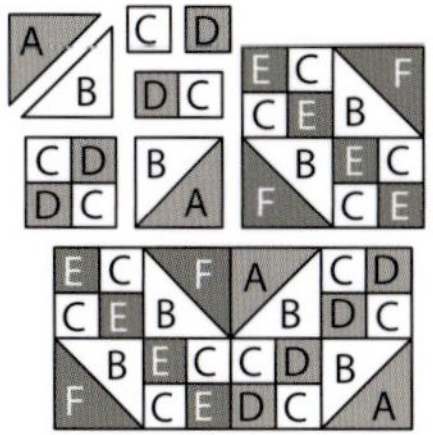

For	Cut	Need	4″	6″	8″	10″	12″
A	2 ■	4 ◪	1⅞	2⅜	2⅞	3⅜	3⅞
B	4 □	8 ◪	1⅞	2⅜	2⅞	3⅜	3⅞
C	16 □	16 □	1	1¼	1½	1¾	2
D	8 ■	8 ■	1	1¼	1½	1¾	2
E	8 ■	8 ■	1	1¼	1½	1¾	2
F	2 ■	4 ◪	1⅞	2⅜	2⅞	3⅜	3⅞

What pieces can I cut from a 10″ or 5″ precut square?

Cutting from 10″ × 10″ Squares

Cut in half to get 2 rectangles 5″ × 10″.

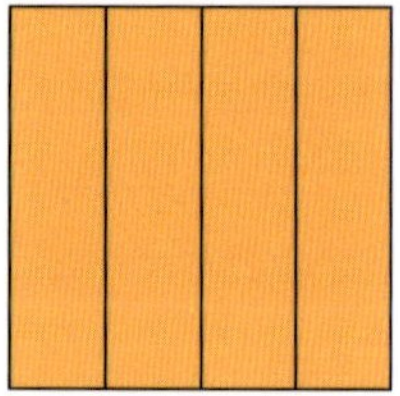

Cut into 4 strips 2½″ × 10″.

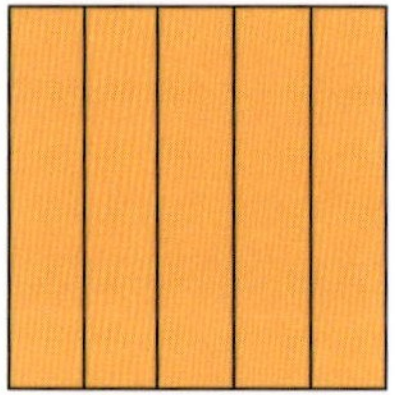

Cut into 5 strips 2″ × 10″.

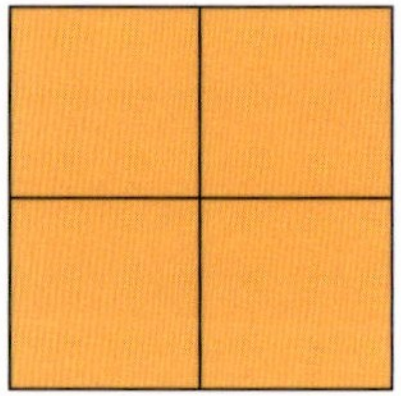

Cut in half twice, to get 4 squares 5″ × 5″.

Cut into 16 squares 2½″ × 2½″ (Mini Charm Squares).

Cut diagonally once to get 2 half-square triangles that, once trimmed, finish to 9″.

Cut diagonally twice to get 4 quarter-square triangles that once trimmed, finish to 8½″.

Cutting from 5″ × 5″ Squares

Cut into 4 squares 2½″ × 2½″.

Cut diagonally once to get 2 half-square triangles that, once trimmed, finish to 4″.

Cut diagonally twice to get 4 quarter-square triangles that, once trimmed, finish to 3½″.

BONUS BLOCK

Millstone

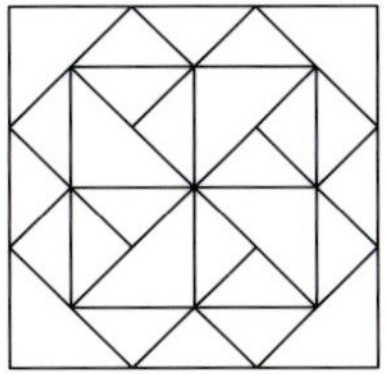

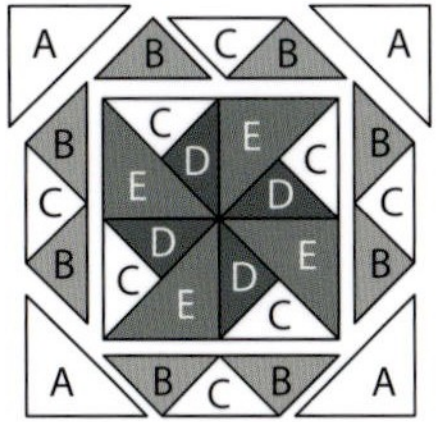

For	Cut	Need	3″	6″	9″	12″	15″
A	2 □	4 ⧄	1⅞	2⅞	3⅞	4⅞	5⅞
B	2 ■	8 ⊠	2¼	3¼	4¼	5¼	6¼
C	2 □	8 ⊠	2¼	3¼	4¼	5¼	6¼
D	1 ■	4 ⊠	2¼	3¼	4¼	5¼	6¼
E	2 ■	4 ⧄	1⅞	2⅞	3⅞	4⅞	5⅞

How can I cut fabric most efficiently?

Cutting Squares from Yardage

When you need to cut a number of pieces from your yardage, it is often most efficient to first cut your fabric into strips, and then cut those strips into squares (or rectangles). It's usually best practice to cut the largest squares you need first, and get progressively smaller. That way you can make the best use of leftover portions of strips by cutting them into the next size down.

The chart tells you how many squares you can cut from one strip of a 40″ width of fabric (so you'll know how many strips you'll need of each size).

SIZE OF SQUARES	# IN 40″	# OF STRIPS in 1 yard
18½″–20″	2	1
13½″–18″	2	2
12½″–13″	3	2
10½″–12″	3	3
10″	4	3
9½″	4	3
9″	4	4
8½″	4	4
8″	5	4
7½″	5	4
7″	5	5

SIZE OF SQUARES	# IN 40″	# OF STRIPS in 1 yard
6½″	6	5
6″	6	6
5½″	7	6
5″	8	7
4½″	8	8
4″	10	9
3½″	11	10
3″	13	12
2½″	16	14
2″	20	18
1½″	26	24

BONUS BLOCK

Monkey Wrench

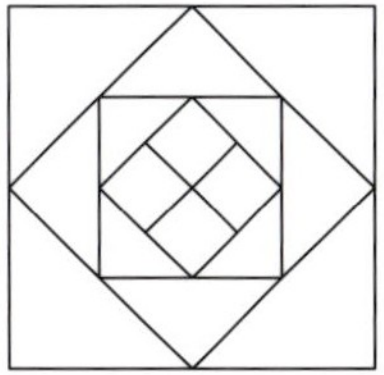  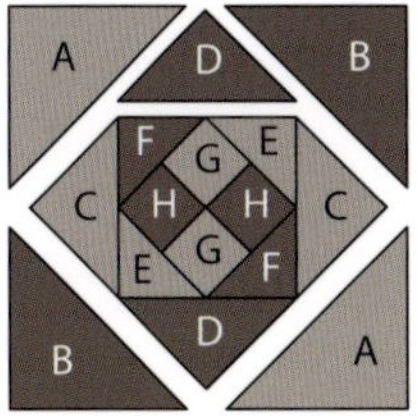

For	Cut	Need	4″	6″	8″	10″	12″
A	1	2	2⅞	3⅞	4⅞	5⅞	6⅞
B	1	2	2⅞	3⅞	4⅞	5⅞	6⅞
C	1	2	3¼	4¼	5¼	6¼	7¼
D	1	2	3¼	4¼	5¼	6¼	7¼
E	1	2	1⅞	2⅜	2⅞	3⅜	3⅞
F	1	2	1⅞	2⅜	2⅞	3⅜	3⅞
G	2	2	1¼	1½	2	2¼	2⅝
H	2	2	1¼	1½	2	2¼	2⅝

15B

What seam allowance should I add when I cut different shapes?

Cutting Numbers for Various Shapes

When you're sewing a ¼″ seam allowance, the cut size (or "unfinished" size) of some pieces are relatively easy to figure out. Add ¼″ to all sides and you have a piece that is ½″ large overall. This math works for squares, rectangles, and strips.

But when you get into other shapes, the math gets more complicated. The next three cards are a cheat sheet to quilting math to save you time and make it easy.

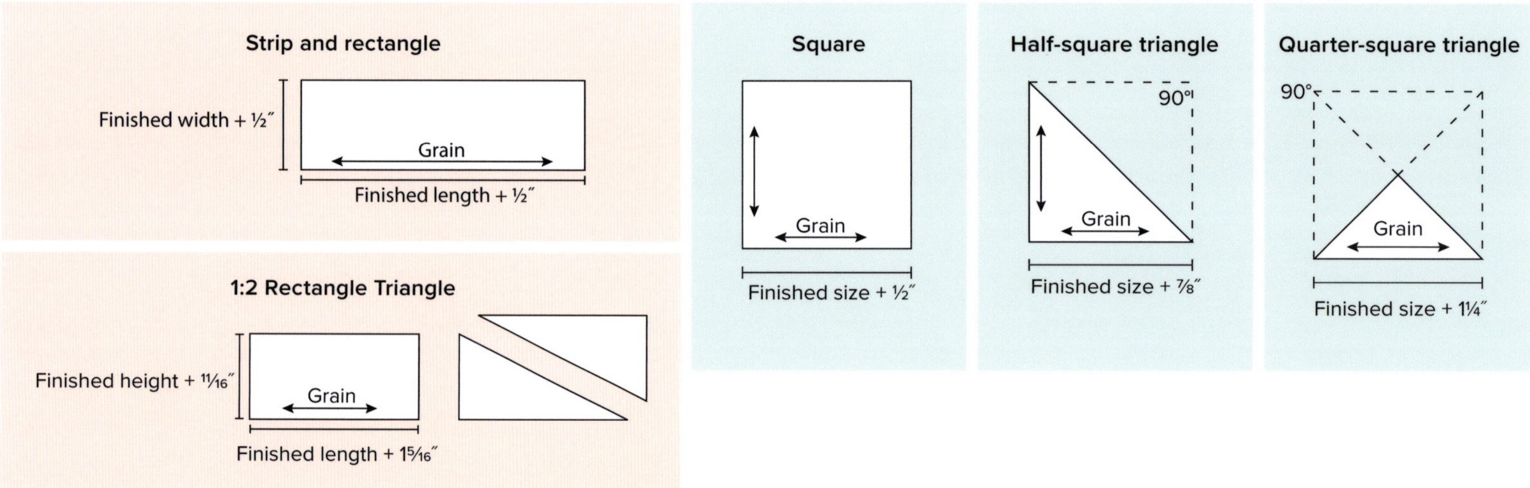

BONUS BLOCK

Night Vision

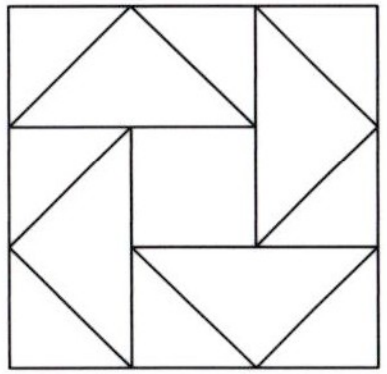

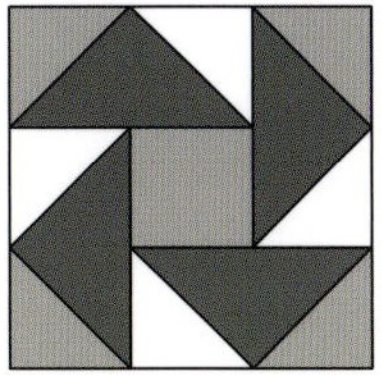

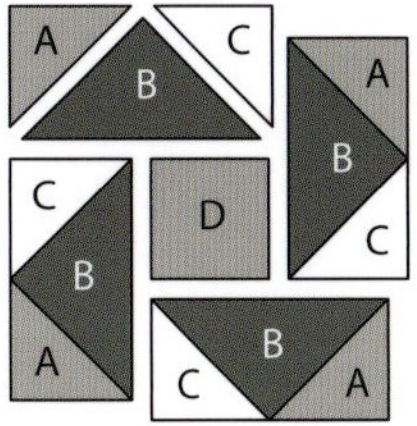

For	Cut	Need	3″	6″	9″	12″	15″
A	2	4	1⅞	2⅞	3⅞	4⅞	5⅞
B	1	4	3¼	5¼	7¼	9¼	11¼
C	2	4	1⅞	2⅞	3⅞	4⅞	5⅞
D	1	1	1½	2½	3½	4½	5½

This block requires that you use partial seams during construction.

45° trapezoid

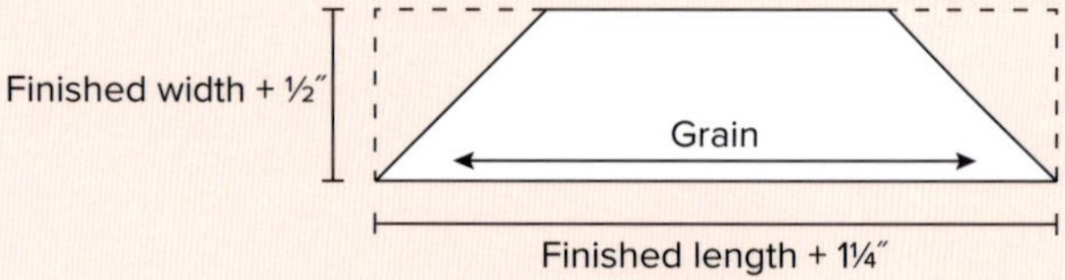

Half 45° trapezoid

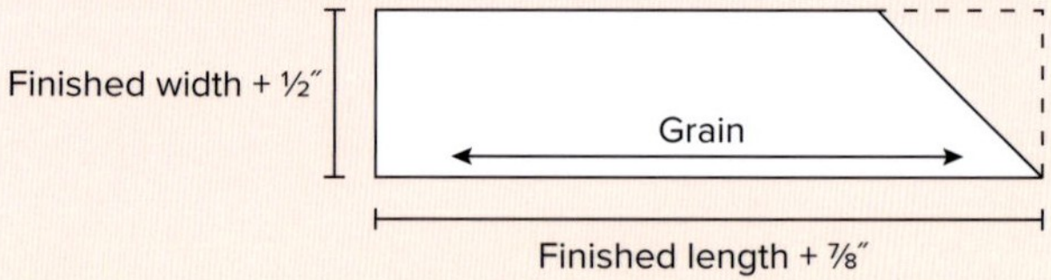

Isosceles triangle

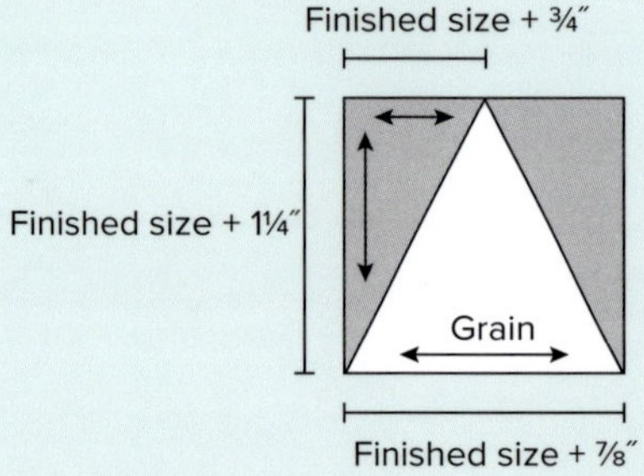

Equilateral triangle

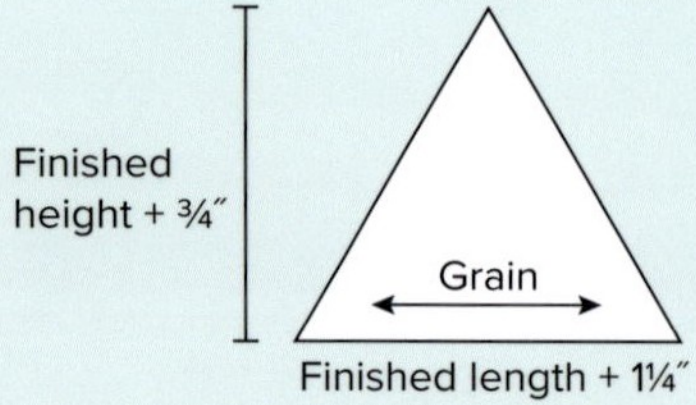

30° diamond

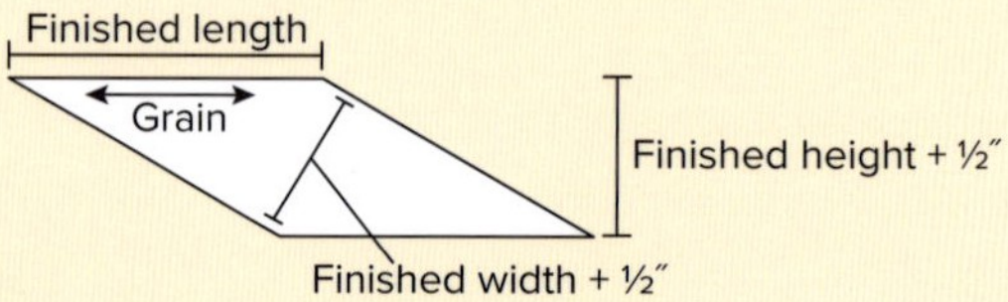

45° diamond

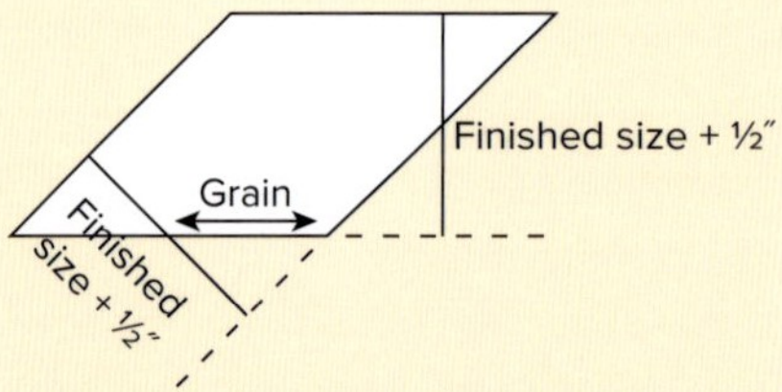

60° diamond

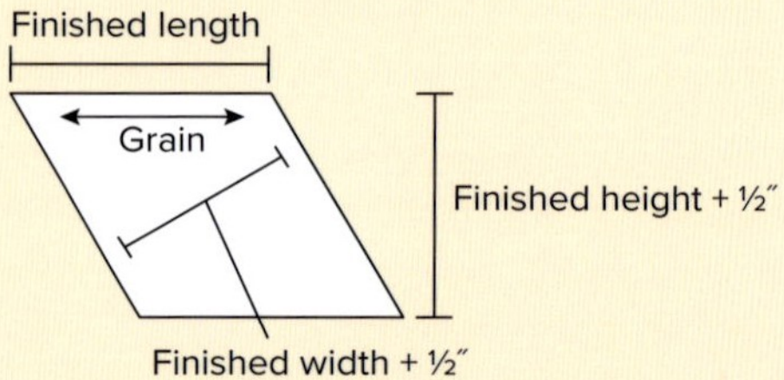

BONUS BLOCK

North Star

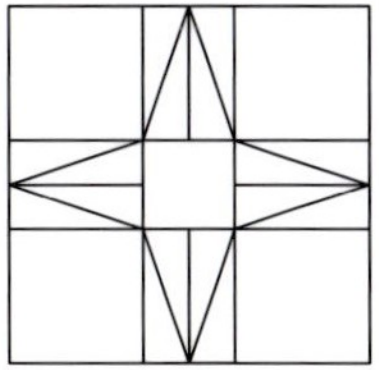

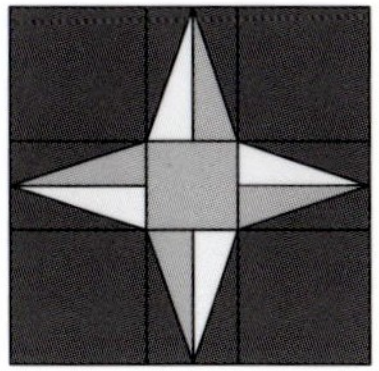

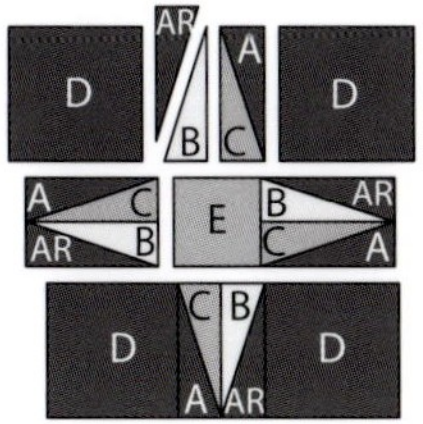

For	Cut	Need	4″	6″	8″	10″	12″
A	2	4	1⅛ × 3⅜	1⅜ × 4⅛	1⅝ × 4⅞	1⅞ × 5⅝	2⅛ × 6⅜
AR	2	4	1⅛ × 3⅜	1⅜ × 4⅛	1⅝ × 4⅞	1⅞ × 5⅝	2⅛ × 6⅜
B	2	4	1⅛ × 3⅜	1⅜ × 4⅛	1⅝ × 4⅞	1⅞ × 5⅝	2⅛ × 6⅜
C	2	4	1⅛ × 3⅜	1⅜ × 4⅛	1⅝ × 4⅞	1⅞ × 5⅝	2⅛ × 6⅜
D	4	4	2	2¾	3½	4¼	5
E	1	1	1½	2	2½	3	3½

Parallelogram

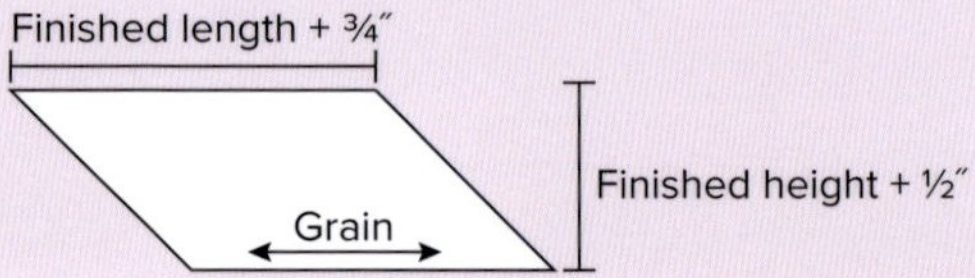

Hexagon

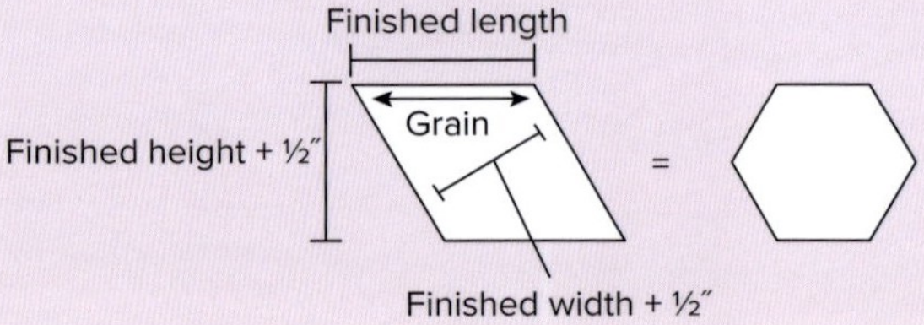

Octagon

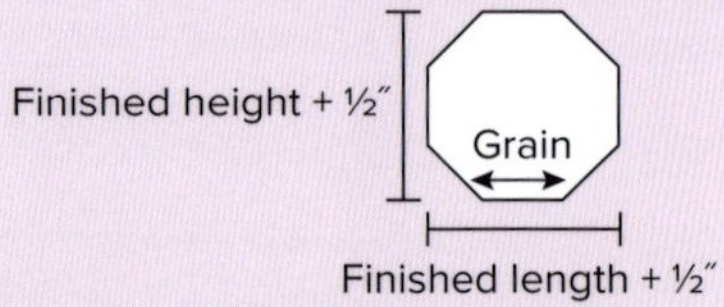

Double prism

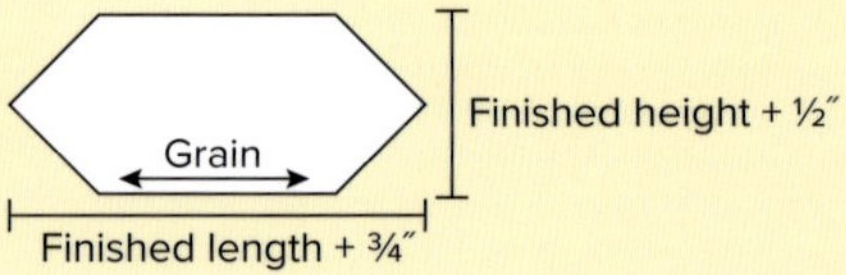

Single prism

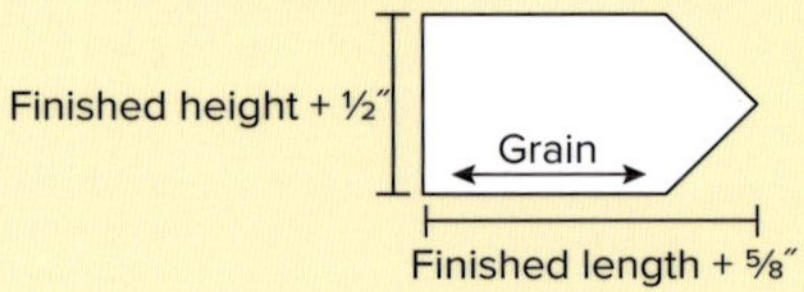

BONUS BLOCK

Old Maid's Puzzle

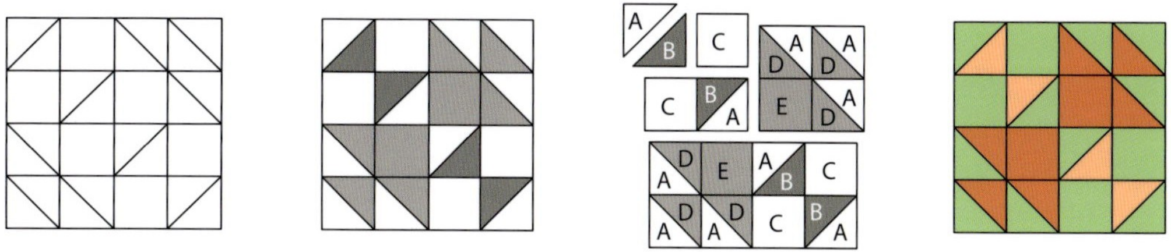

For	Cut	Need	4″	6″	8″	10″	12″
A	5 □	10 ⧄	1⅞	2⅜	2⅞	3⅜	3⅞
B	2 ■	4 ⧄	1⅞	2⅜	2⅞	3⅜	3⅞
C	4 □	4 □	1½	2	2½	3	3½
D	3 ■	6 ⧄	1⅞	2⅜	2⅞	3⅜	3⅞
E	2 ■	2 ■	1½	2	2½	3	3½

How can I save time and sew more than one half-square triangle unit at the same time?

Half-Square Triangle Units—Method 1: Sew and Slice, Two at a Time

In this method, you sew 2 oversized squares together, cut them apart, press them, and trim them to size. This eliminates sewing a cut bias edge. You get 2 half-square triangle units from each set of squares.

1. Cut 2 squares 1″ larger than finished size of desired finished triangle unit. Place squares right sides together and draw a diagonal line from corner to corner. Draw stitching lines ¼″ on each side of centerline.

2. Stitch on each of the 2 stitching lines. Press.

3. Cut on centerline.

4. Press open with both seam allowances to one side. Trim to size, including seam allowance.

1

2

3

4

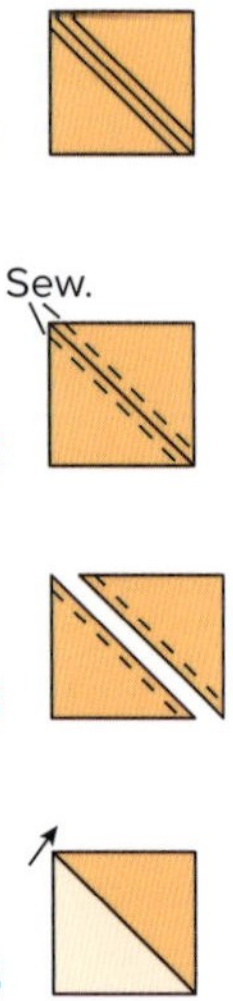

BONUS BLOCK

Paradox

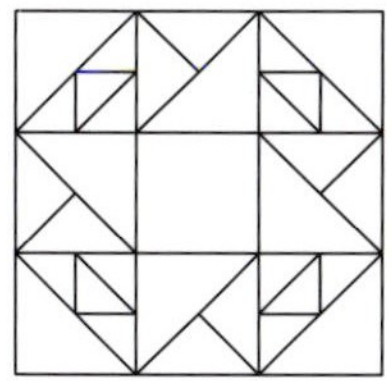

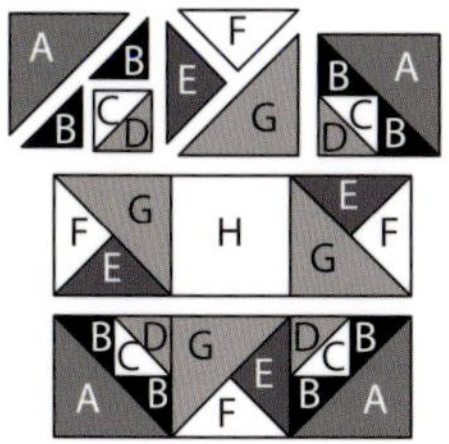

For	Cut	Need	3″	6″	9″	12″	15″
A	2 ■	4 ◪	1⅞	2⅞	3⅞	4⅞	5⅞
B	4 ■	8 ◪	1⅜	1⅞	2⅜	2⅞	3⅜
C	2 □	4 ◸	1⅜	1⅞	2⅜	2⅞	3⅜
D	2 ■	4 ◪	1⅜	1⅞	2⅜	2⅞	3⅜
E	1 ■	4 ⊠	2¼	3¼	4¼	5¼	6¼
F	1 □	4 ⊠	2¼	3¼	4¼	5¼	6¼
G	2 ■	4 ◪	1⅞	2⅞	3⅞	4⅞	5⅞
H	1 □	1 □	1½	2½	3½	4½	5½

Half-Square Triangle Units—Method 2: Eight From a Square

This is a fun and fast way to make 8 half-square triangle units at a time. Refer to the following chart for sizes.

SIZE TO CUT LARGE SQUARES (Inches)	TRIMMED HALF-SQUARE TRIANGLE UNIT SIZE (Inches)	FINISHED SIZE (Inches)
4	1½	1
5	2	1½
6	2½	2
7	3	2½
8	3½	3
9	4	3½
10	4½	4
11	5	4½
12	5½	5
13	6	5½
14	6½	6

1. Cut 2 squares and place them right sides together. Draw diagonal lines from corner to corner in both directions. Draw stitching lines ¼″ on each side of diagonal lines.

2. Stitch on each of the 4 stitching lines. Press. Then cut as shown in red.

3. Cut on drawn diagonal lines.

4. Press open with both seam allowances to one side. Trim to size, including seam allowance.

1

2
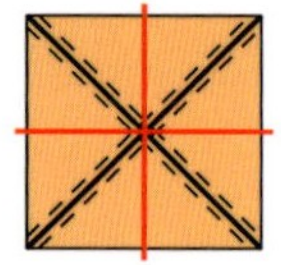

3
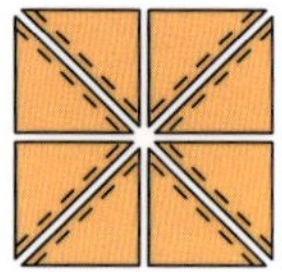

4
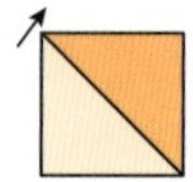

BONUS BLOCK

Pine Tree

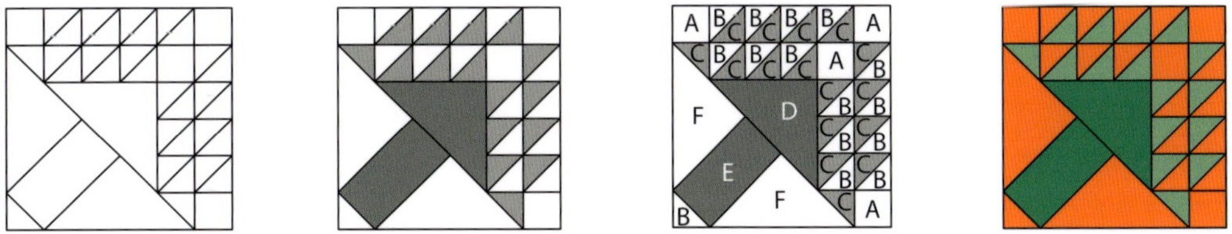

For	Cut	Need	3″	6″	9″	12″	15″
A	4 □	4 □	1	1½	2	2½	3
B	8 □	15 ⧄	1⅜	1⅞	2⅜	2⅞	3⅜
C	8 ■	16 ⧄	1⅜	1⅞	2⅜	2⅞	3⅜
D	1 ■	1 ⧄	2⅜	3⅞	5⅜	6⅞	8⅜
E	1 ▬	1 ▬	1¼ × 2	1⅞ × 3⅜	2⅝ × 4¾	3⅜ × 6⅛	4 × 7½
F	1 □	2 ⊠	3¼	5¼	7¼	9¼	11¼

Half-Square Triangle Units—Method 3: Sheeting Triangles

This method was created by Barbara Johannah and Ernest Haight independently in the early 1970s.

1. Place 2 fabrics right sides together. Draw vertical parallel lines on fabric, spaced the finished size of the squares you desire + ⅞″ (for example, 2⅞″ for a finished 2″ square).

2. Draw horizontal parallel lines the same distance apart as the vertical lines.

3. Draw diagonal lines in every other square, starting in a corner.

4. Draw diagonal lines in opposite direction in remaining empty squares. Pin in every blank space.

5. Stitch in a continuous line in the direction of the arrows, ¼″ from the lines, using the same side of the presser foot all the time. Continue sewing until all the diagonal lines have stitching on both sides. Cut apart on all the drawn lines. Press.

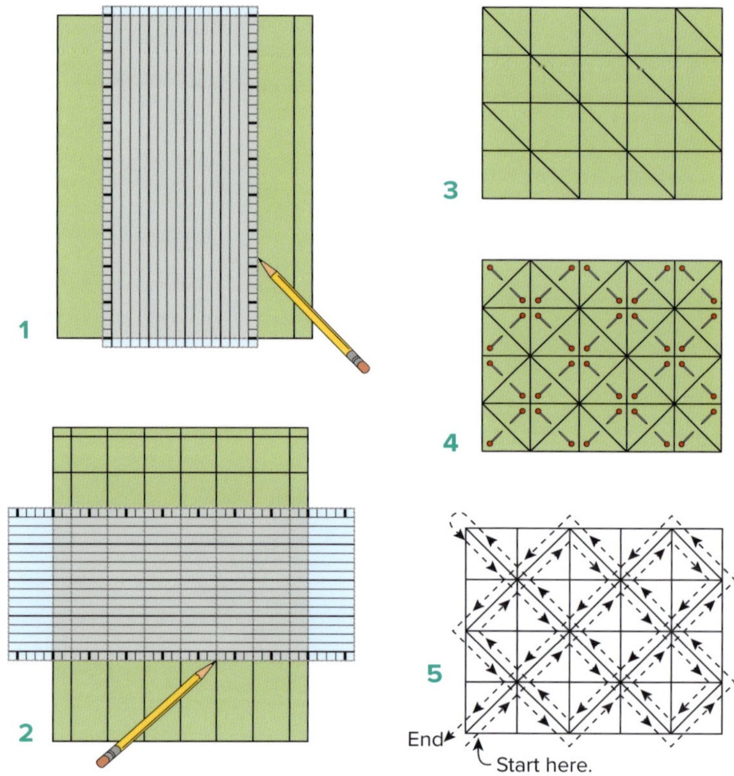

BONUS BLOCK

Poinsettia

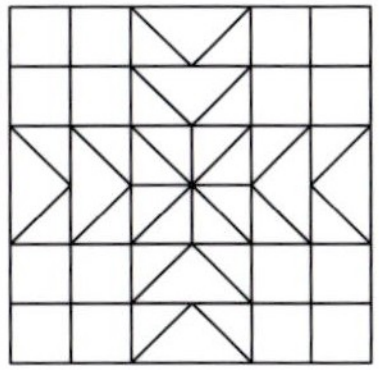

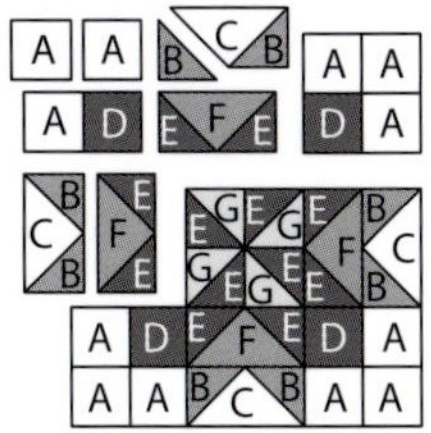

For	Cut	Need	3″	6″	9″	12″	15″
A	12	12	1	1½	2	2½	3
B	4	8	1⅜	1⅞	2⅜	2⅞	3⅜
C	1	4	2¼	3¼	4¼	5¼	6¼
D	4	4	1	1½	2	2½	3
E	6	12	1⅜	1⅞	2⅜	2⅞	3⅜
F	1	4	2¼	3¼	4¼	5¼	6¼
G	2	4	1⅜	1⅞	2⅜	2⅞	3⅜

▶ *What are the tricks to sewing together Flying Geese?*

Cutting Numbers for Stitch-And-Flip Flying Geese

FINISHED BLOCK SIZE (Inches)	RECTANGLE FOR CENTER TRIANGLE (Inches)	SQUARES FOR CORNER TRIANGLES (Inches)
1 × 2	1½ × 2½	1½
1½ × 3	2 × 3½	2
2 × 4	2½ × 4½	2½
2½ × 5	3 × 5½	3
3 × 6	3½ × 6½	3½
3½ × 7	4 × 7½	4
4 × 8	4½ × 8½	4½

1. Lightly draw a diagonal line from 1 corner to opposite corner on wrong sides of 2 squares.

2. With right sides together, place a square on end of rectangle.

3. Sew directly on line, trim seam allowance to ¼″, and press open.

4. With right sides together, place other square on other end of rectangle. Sew directly on line, trim seam allowance to ¼″, and press open.

1
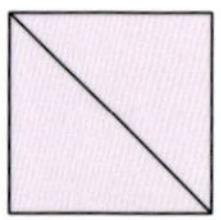

2
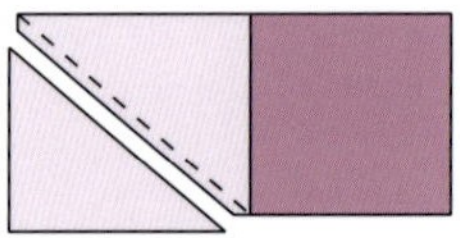

3
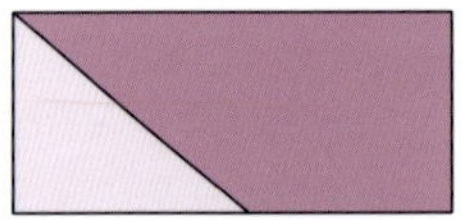

4
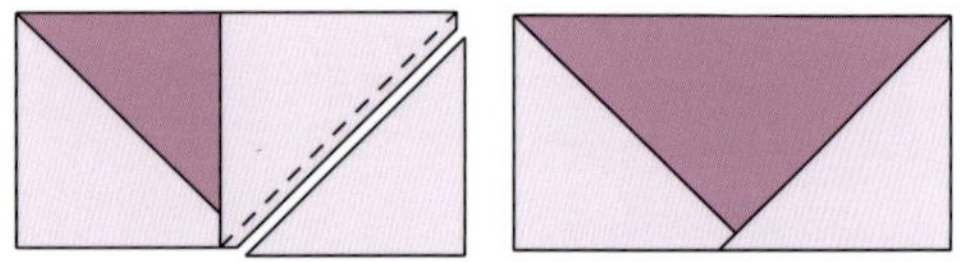

BONUS BLOCK

Rite of Spring

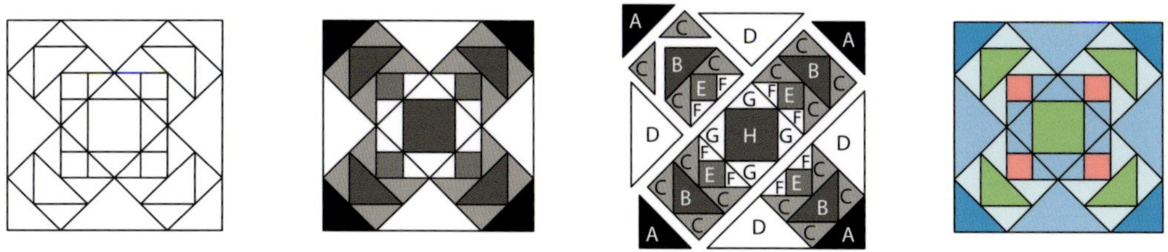

For	Cut	Need	4″	6″	8″	10″	12″
A	2	4	1⅞	2⅜	2⅞	3⅜	3⅞
B	2	4	1⅞	2⅜	2⅞	3⅜	3⅞
C	4	16	2¼	2¾	3¼	3¾	4¼
D	1	4	3¼	4¼	5¼	6¼	7¼
E	4	4	1	1¼	1½	1¾	2
F	4	8	1⅜	1⅝	1⅞	2⅛	2⅜
G	1	4	2¼	2¾	3¼	3¾	4¼
H	1	1	1½	2	2½	3	3½

Cutting Numbers for Four-at-a-Time Flying Geese

BLOCK SIZE (Inches)	LARGE SQUARE (Inches)	SMALL SQUARES (Inches)
1 × 2	3¼	1⅞
1½ × 3	4¼	2⅜
2 × 4	5¼	2⅞
2½ × 5	6¼	3⅜
3 × 6	7¼	3⅞
3½ × 7	8¼	4⅜
4 × 8	9¼	4⅞

1. With right sides together, position small squares on large square. Draw centerline from corner to corner on small squares and pin.

2. Stitch a scant ¼″ from each side of line. Cut unit in half on centerline.

3. Press open.

4. With right sides together, place another small square on the bottom of large triangle. Draw line from corner to corner on small square and pin. Stitch a scant ¼″ from each side of line.

5. Cut unit in half on drawn line and press open. Repeat Step 4 for remaining piece.

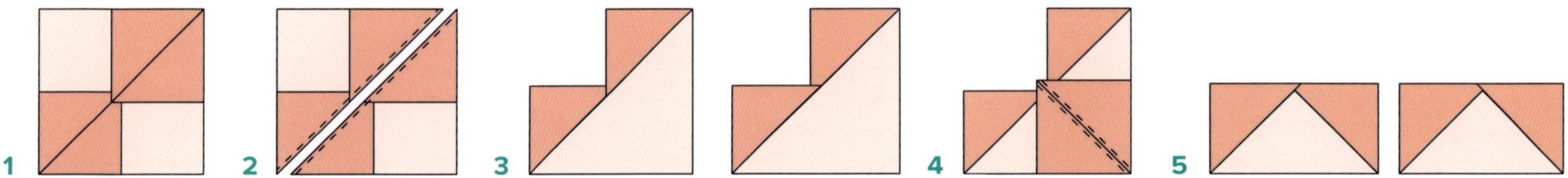

BONUS BLOCK

Road to California

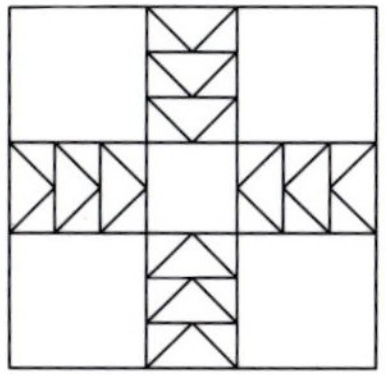

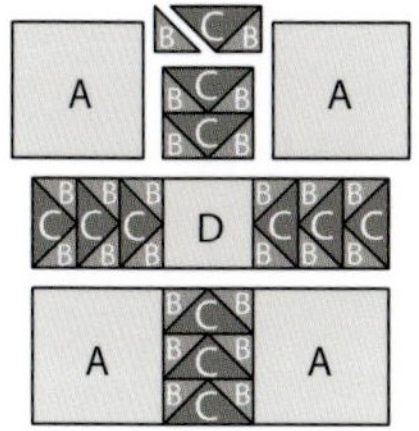

For	Cut	Need	4″	6″	8″	10″	12″
A	4	4	2	2¾	3½	4¼	5
B	12	24	1⅜	1⅝	1⅞	2⅛	2⅜
C	3	12	2¼	2¾	3¼	3¾	4¼
D	1	1	1½	2	2½	3	3½

▶ *Can you save me time and do the math for a Square-in-a-Square block?*

Cutting Numbers For Square-in-a-Square Block

FINISHED BLOCK SIZE (Inches)	CENTER SQUARE (Inches)	CORNER SQUARES (Inches)
1	1¼	1⅜
1½	1½	1⅝
2	1⅞	1⅞
2½	2¼	2⅛
3	2⅝	2⅜
3½	3	2⅝
4	3⅜	2⅞
4½	3⅝	3⅛
5	4	3⅜
5½	4⅜	3⅝
6	4¾	3⅞

1. Cut 2 corner squares in half diagonally.

2. With right sides together, center the long side of 1 triangle on an edge of center square. Pin and stitch. Position the second triangle on the opposite side of the center square. Pin and stitch.

3. Press open.

4. Repeat Steps 2 and 3.

1

2

3
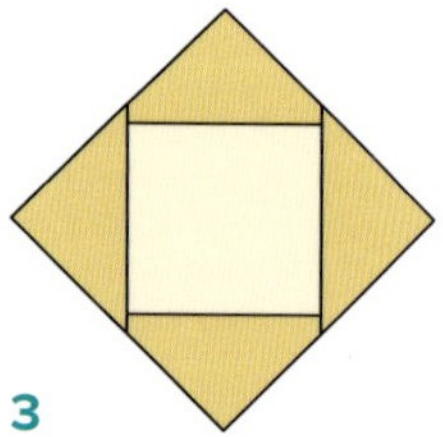

BONUS BLOCK

Rolling Stone

For	Cut	Need	3″	6″	9″	12″	15″
A	4 □	4 □	1¼	2	2⅝	3⅜	4
B	8 ■	16 ◩	1⅜	1⅞	2⅜	2⅞	3⅜
C	4 ▬	4 ▬	1 × 1½	1½ × 2½	2 × 3½	2½ × 4½	3 × 5½
D	4 ▭	4 ▭	1 × 1½	1½ × 2½	2 × 3½	2½ × 4½	3 × 5½
E	1 ■	1 ■	1½	2½	3½	4½	5½

▶ *How do I sew half-rectangle triangles? Aren't they like HSTs?*

Half-Rectangle Triangles

Half-rectangle triangles (HRTs) are not like half-square triangles. The main difference is that these shapes are directional. You can have right-leaning HRTs and left-leaning HRTs. When cutting out the shapes and sewing them together, you need to be aware of which one you need—left or right leaning—or your pattern might be wrong.

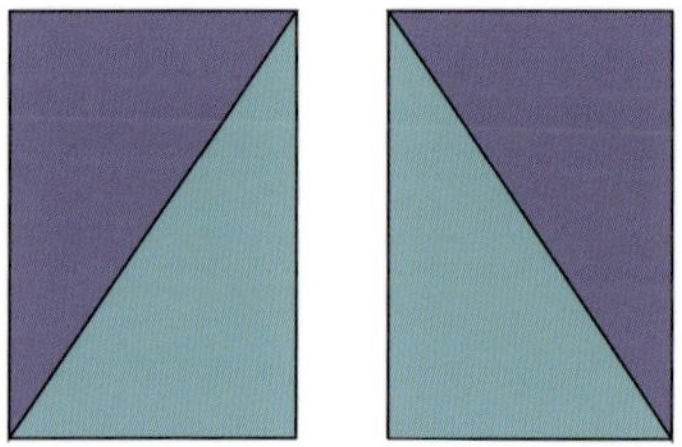

HRTS FROM RECTANGLES, ONE AND TWO AT A TIME

There are two ways to make it easier to sew your HRTs. The first is to cut your pieces larger than needed and trim down the HRT units. The second is to make them with rectangles and not from triangles.

Draw a line corner to corner on the wrong side of 1 rectangle and place your rectangles right sides together. To sew 1 HST unit, sew on the drawn line and trim away the excess from 1 side. To sew 2 HST units, sew ¼″ away from both sides of the line and trim on the line.

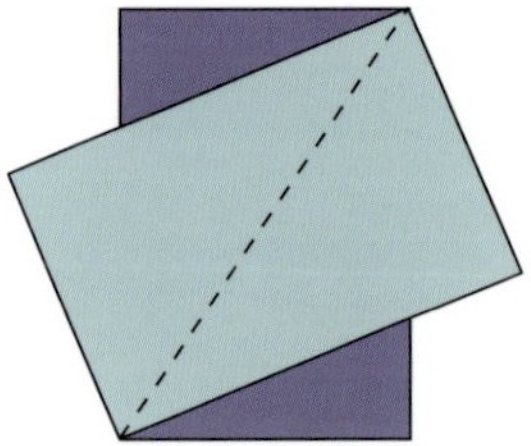

Sew 1 HRT.

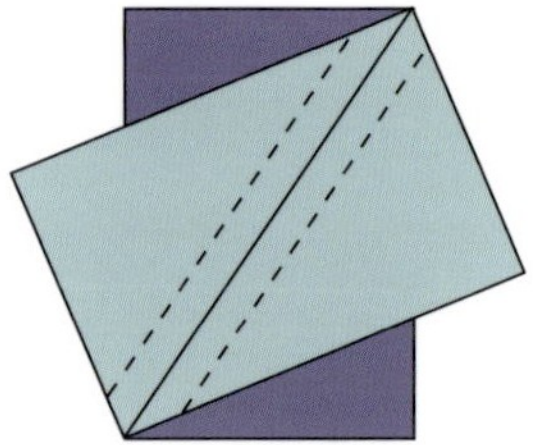

Sew 2 HRTs.

BONUS BLOCK

Sawtooth Patchwork

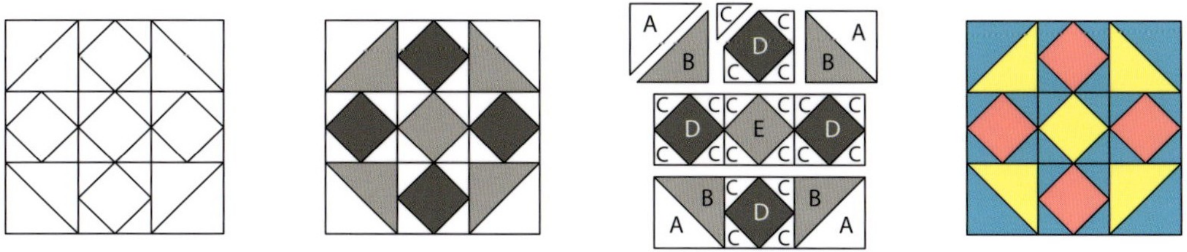

For	Cut	Need	3″	6″	9″	12″	15″
A	2 □	4 ⧄	1⅞	2⅞	3⅞	4⅞	5⅞
B	2 ■	4 ⧄	1⅞	2⅞	3⅞	4⅞	5⅞
C	10 □	20 ⧄	1⅜	1⅞	2⅜	2⅞	3⅜
D	4 ■	4 ■	1¼	2	2⅝	3⅜	4
E	1 ■	1 ■	1¼	2	2⅝	3⅜	4

HRTS FROM TRIANGLES

To line up your triangles when sewing HRT units from triangles and not rectangles, the trick is to get your pieces offset correctly. Your pieces should overlap where the edge of 1 angled edge of 1 piece hits the flat bottom of the other piece at the ¼″ stitching line. The offset of the 2 pieces—as seen in the length of the equal bunny ears sticking out on the edges of the overlapped pieces of fabric—vary depending on the proportions of your triangles. Narrow triangles result in long bunny ears because it takes a larger overlap before the ¼″ is reached.

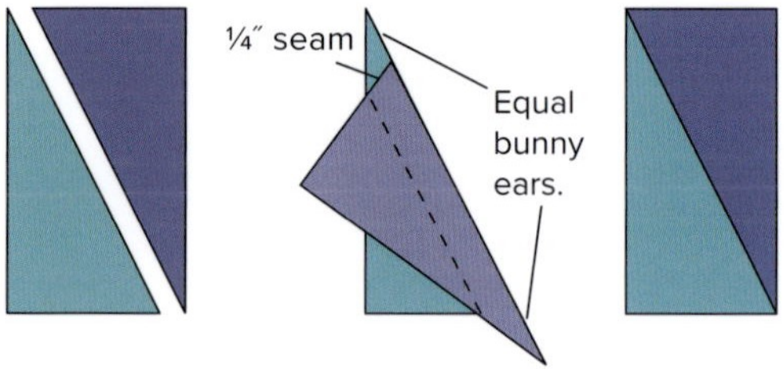

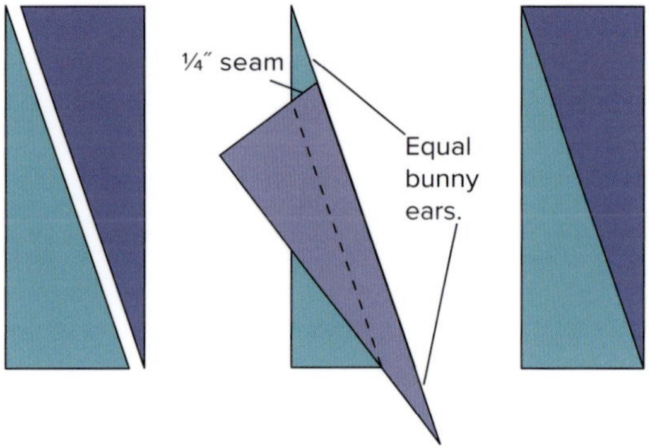

BONUS BLOCK

Shoofly

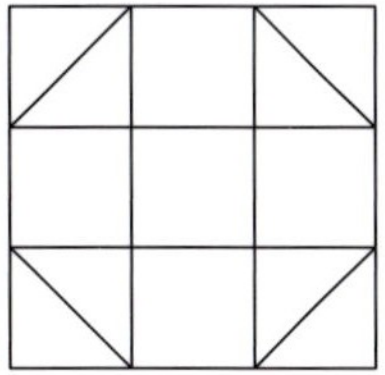

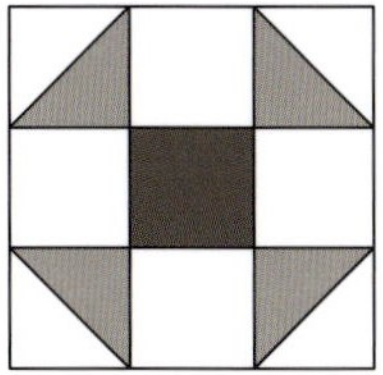

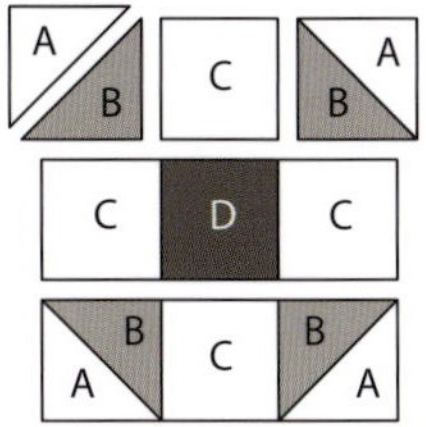

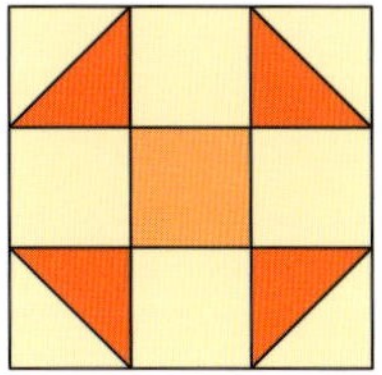

For	Cut	Need	3″	6″	9″	12″	15″
A	2 □	4 ⧄	1⅞	2⅞	3⅞	4⅞	5⅞
B	2 ■	4 ⧄	1⅞	2⅞	3⅞	4⅞	5⅞
C	4 □	4 □	1½	2½	3½	4½	5½
D	1 ■	1 ■	1½	2½	3½	4½	5½

How do I get my shapes to line up when sewing them together?

Corner Alignment for Piecing Shapes

Some shapes are easy to sew together. Squares to squares? Obviously that's no problem. Other shapes, it's not always as easy to remember what edges should line up.

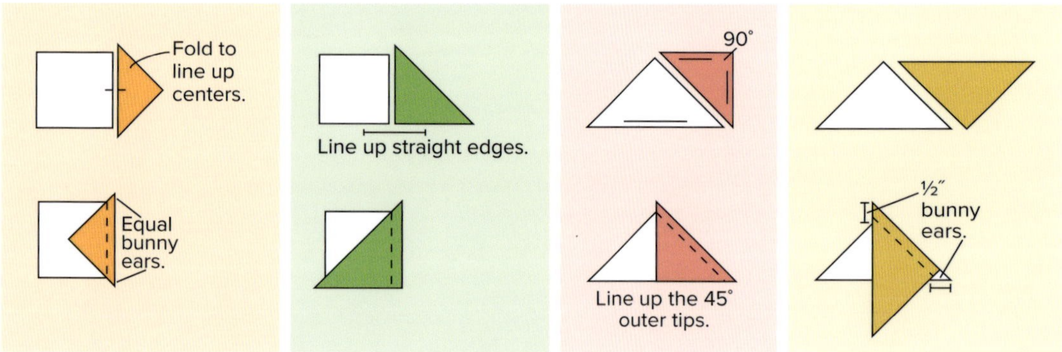

Courtesy of Alex Anderson; reprinted from *Simply Stars* (from C&T Publishing)

Sewing Squares to Squares

1. Place the squares right sides together.

2. Sew diagonally from corner to corner.

3. Trim and press.

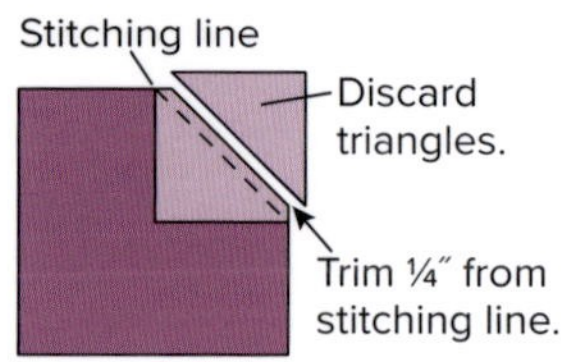

BONUS BLOCK

Single Wedding Ring

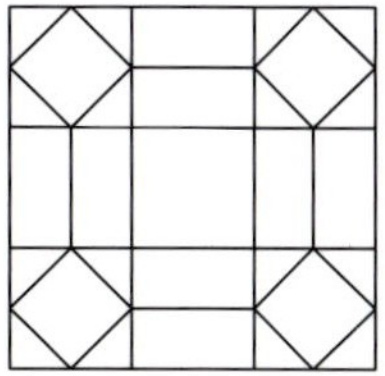

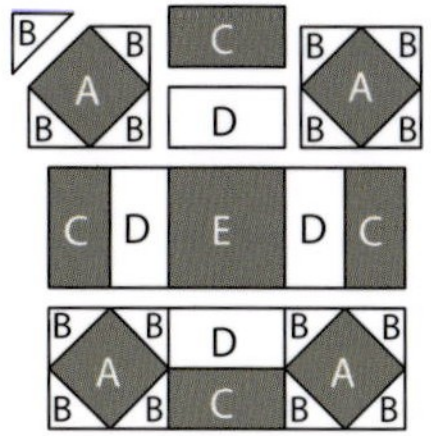

For	Cut	Need	3″	6″	9″	12″	15″
A	4 ■	4 ■	1¼	2	2⅝	3⅜	4
B	8 □	16 ⧄	1⅜	1⅞	2⅜	2⅞	3⅜
C	4 ▬	4 ▬	1 × 1½	1½ × 2½	2 × 3½	2½ × 4½	3 × 5½
D	4 ▭	4 ▭	1 × 1½	1½ × 2½	2 × 3½	2½ × 4½	3 × 5½
E	1 ■	1 ■	1½	2½	3½	4½	5½

How do I sew Y-seams?

Y-Seam Construction

1. Units ready for piecing

2. Shows piece letters and seam sewing order

3. Place piece C on top of piece A and sew seam #1 from edge to edge.

4. Finger-press seam allowance as shown by arrow.

5. Place piece B on top of piece C. Flip pieces over so piece C is on top. Start sewing seam #2 at outer point and stop at previous stitch line. Lock stitches with either a lockstitch or backstitch.

6. Bring the remaining 2 edges together and sew from the point to the previous stitching line, locking the stitches at both ends. Press.

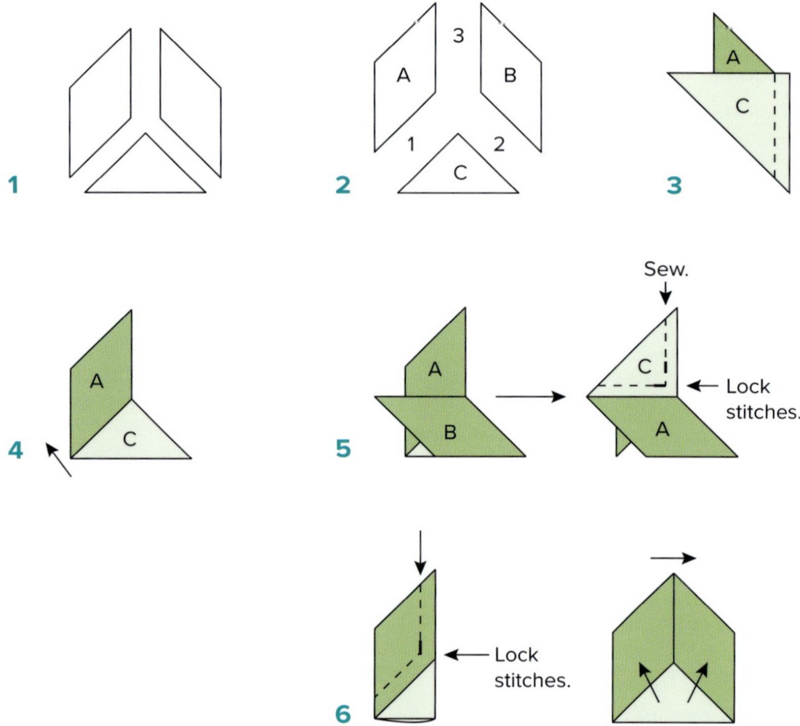

BONUS BLOCK

Snowflake

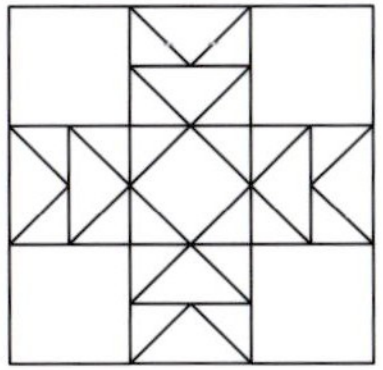

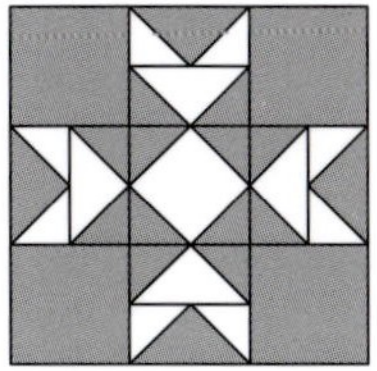

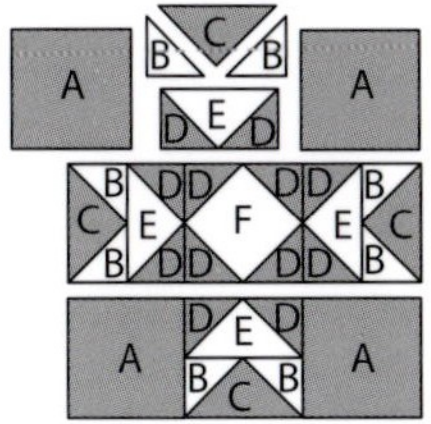

For	Cut	Need	3″	6″	9″	12″	15″
A	4 ■	4 ■	1½	2½	3½	4½	5½
B	4 □	8 ⧄	1⅜	1⅞	2⅜	2⅞	3⅜
C	1 ■	4 ⊠	2¼	3¼	4¼	5¼	6¼
D	6 ■	12 ⧄	1⅜	1⅞	2⅜	2⅞	3⅜
E	1 □	4 ⊠	2¼	3¼	4¼	5¼	6¼
F	1 □	1 □	1¼	1⅞	2⅝	3⅜	4

Curved-Seam Construction

Sewing curved seams is easier than you'd expect. Here are a few options as well as a few tips to keep you moving. The key is to go slow and keep your cool. And keep your sense of humor. Try it on some scraps first so you can have fun with it!

REGISTRATION MARKS: METHOD 1

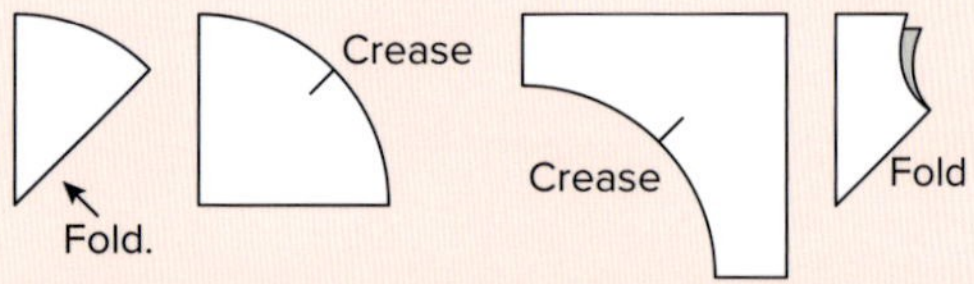

Fold fabric in half to form crease line.

PIECING WITH A CONVEX SHAPE ON TOP

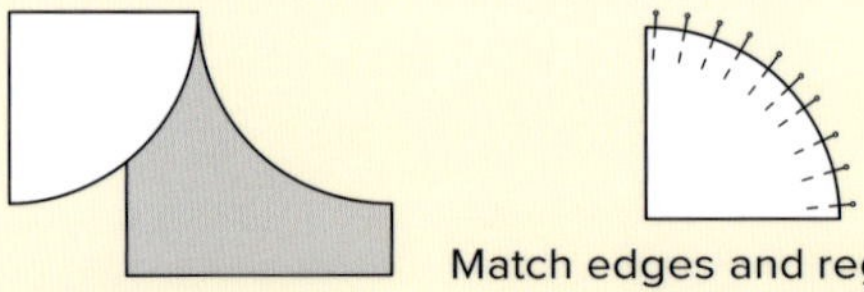

Match corners.

Match edges and registration marks and pin. Then stitch.

REGISTRATION MARKS: METHOD 2

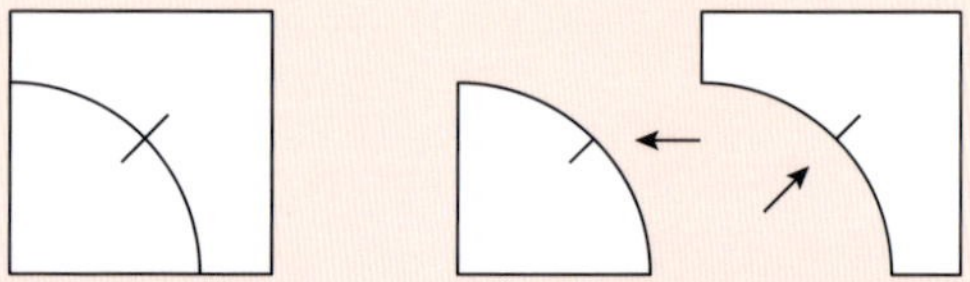

Mark registration marks on templates.

Mark registration marks on fabric with pencil or cut ⅛″ into seam allowance.

PIECING WITH A CONCAVE SHAPE ON TOP

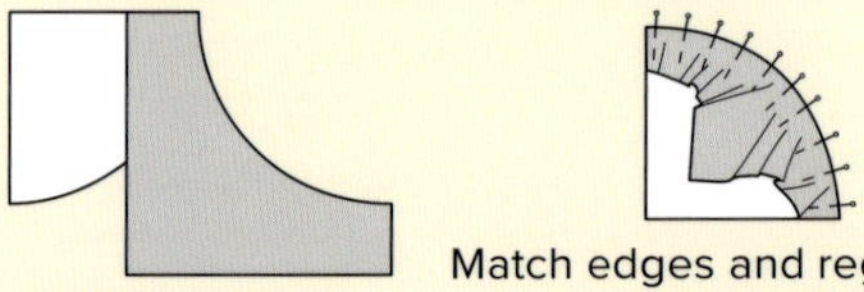

Match corners.

Match edges and registration marks and pin. Then stitch.

TIPS

To ensure success, follow these suggestions:

- Lengthen your stitch slightly.
- Stitch slowly to control the fabric.
- Use the needle-down feature on your sewing machine (if available).
- Keep the fabric edges together.
- Sew an accurate ¼″ seam allowance.

BONUS BLOCK

Spinning Star

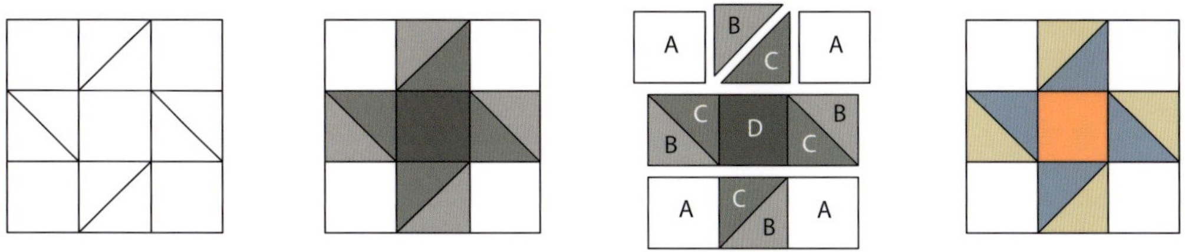

For	Cut	Need	3″	6″	9″	12″	15″
A	4 □	4 □	1½	2½	3½	4½	5½
B	2 □	4 ⧄	1⅞	2⅞	3⅞	4⅞	5⅞
C	2 □	4 ⧄	1⅞	2⅞	3⅞	4⅞	5⅞
D	1 □	1 □	1½	2½	3½	4½	5½

▶ *How do I miter my quilt borders?*

Mitered Border Corner Construction

1. Pin securely and stitch strips to quilt top; start and stop stitching ¼″ from quilt edge.

2. Press borders open and extend excess border length beyond each end.

3. Position border strips for mitering.

4. Fold top border strip under so it meets edge of bottom border strip and forms a 45° angle. Press the fold in place.

5. Pin the fold in place. Position a 90° angle ruler over corner until it is flat and square. Remove pins and press the fold firmly. Center masking tape over mitered fold.

6. Turn quilt top over. Draw a line slightly outside crease. Fold center section of quilt top diagonally from corner, right sides together, and align long edges of border strips. Beginning at inside corner, backstitch and stitch on line. Backstitch at end. Remove tape, trim seam allowance to ¼″, and press seam open.

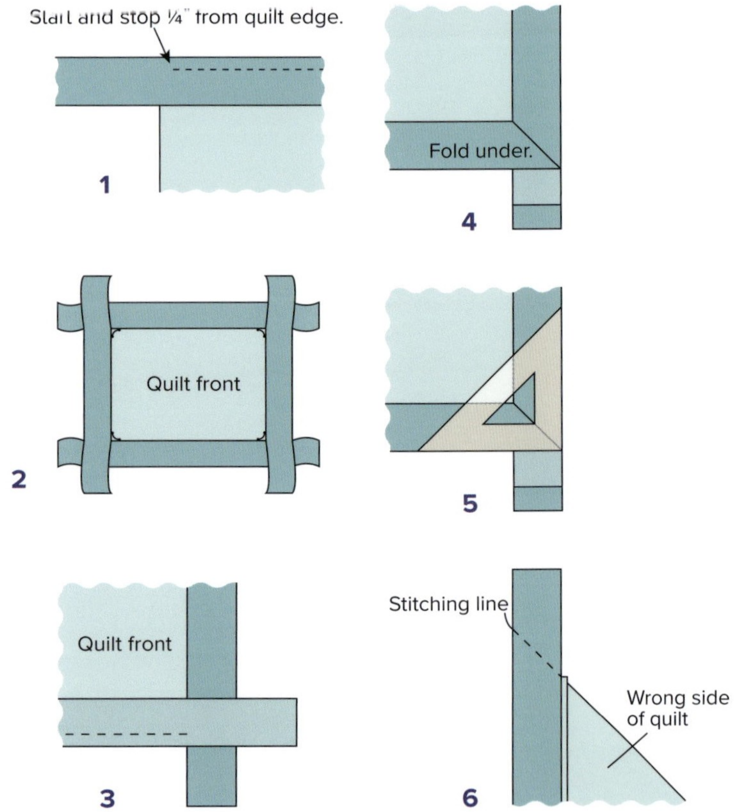

BONUS BLOCK

Spools

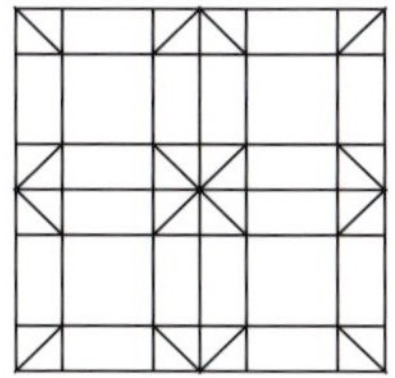

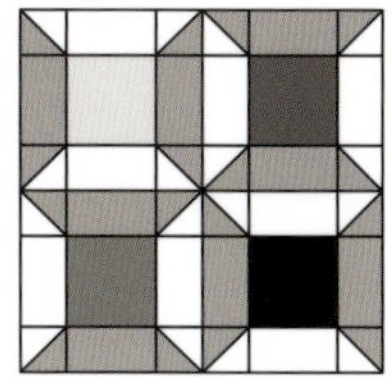

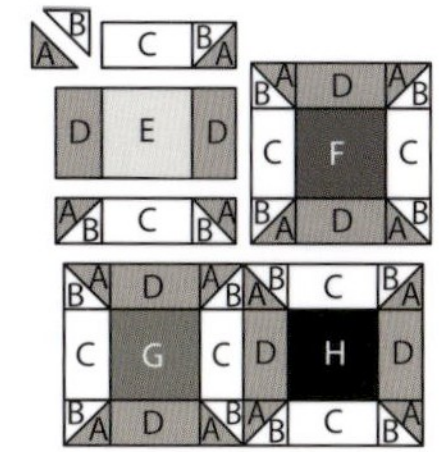

For	Cut	Need	4″	6″	8″	10″	12″
A	8	16	1⅜	1⅝	1⅞	2⅛	2⅜
B	8	16	1⅜	1⅝	1⅞	2⅛	2⅜
C	8	8	1 × 1½	1¼ × 2	1½ × 2½	1¾ × 3	2 × 3½
D	8	8	1 × 1½	1¼ × 2	1½ × 2½	1¾ × 3	2 × 3½
E	1	1	1½	2	2½	3	3½
F	1	1	1½	2	2½	3	3½
G	1	1	1½	2	2½	3	3½
H	1	1	1½	2	2½	3	3½

Yardage for Quilt Backing

There are lots of ways to sew together your quilt backing. In a perfect world, your quilt will be close to one, two, or three widths of fabric to make it easy to piece and result in little waste. You can also get creative and piece your backing from scraps and left-over blocks. The table on page 32 is a simple solution using complete lengths of fabric. Unless you luck into a perfect scenario, it will likely lead to leftover fabric that you can use for other projects.

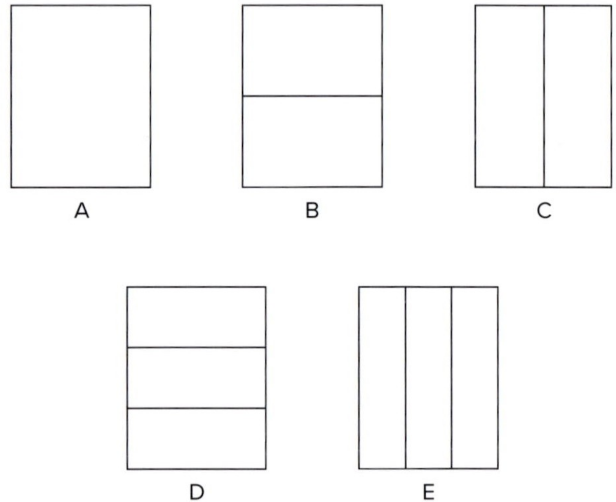

BONUS BLOCK

Star of Hope

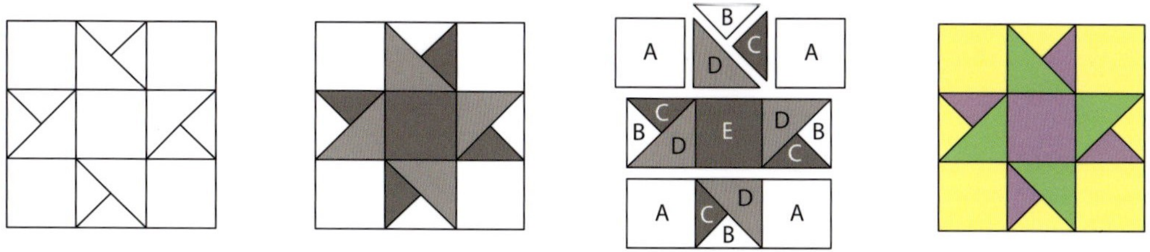

For	Cut	Need	3″	6″	9″	12″	15″
A	4 □	4 □	1½	2½	3½	4½	5½
B	1 □	4 ⊠	2¼	3¼	4¼	5¼	6¼
C	1 ■	4 ⊠	2¼	3¼	4¼	5¼	6¼
D	2 ■	4 ◪	1⅞	2⅞	3⅞	4⅞	5⅞
E	1 ■	1 ■	1½	2½	3½	4½	5½

BACKING SIZE (Inches; Width × Length)	LAYOUT	YARDS
28 × 28	A	1
28 × 40	A	1
34 × 44	A	1¼
40 × 52	A	1½
42 × 56	A	1⅝
48 × 54	B	2¾
48 × 60	B	2¾
52 × 52	B	3
56 × 68	B	3⅛
58 × 62	B	3¼
60 × 72	B	3⅜
60 × 80	B	3⅜
62 × 86	C	4⅞
62 × 92	C	5⅛
66 × 105	C	5⅞

BACKING SIZE (Inches; Width × Length)	LAYOUT	YARDS
69 × 96	C	5⅜
76 × 110	C	6⅛
86 × 105	D	7¼
86 × 115	D	7¼
90 × 110	D	7½
96 × 110	D	8
100 × 111	D	8⅜
106 × 116	D	8⅞
112 × 110	E	9¼
124 × 116	E	9¾

Yardage amounts are based on 42″ fabric width and are rounded up to the nearest ⅛ yard. If your fabric is wider or narrower than 42″, make adjustments accordingly.

For Layout A, we advise purchasing ⅛ yard extra to allow for variations in cutting.

For Layouts B–E, we advise purchasing ¼ yard extra to allow for variations in cutting.

Layouts B and C: Cut the fabric in half crosswise (selvage to selvage), remove the selvages, and then sew the 2 pieces together lengthwise (along the long edges).

Layouts D and E: Cut the fabric in thirds crosswise (selvage to selvage), remove the selvages, and then sew the 3 pieces together lengthwise (along the long edges).

BONUS BLOCK

Star of Sedona

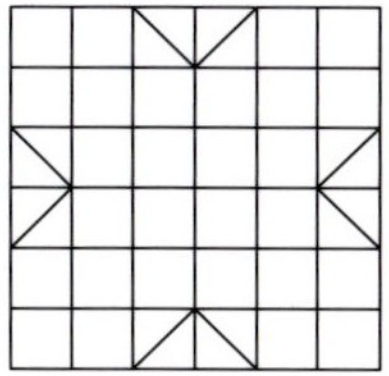

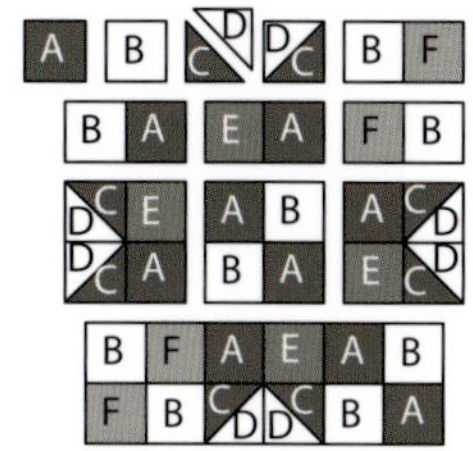

For	Cut	Need	3″	6″	9″	12″	15″
A	10 ■	10 ■	1	1½	2	2½	3
B	10 □	10 □	1	1½	2	2½	3
C	4 ■	8 ◪	1⅜	1⅞	2⅜	2⅞	3⅜
D	4 □	8 ◪	1⅜	1⅞	2⅜	2⅞	3⅜
E	4 ■	4 ■	1	1½	2	2½	3
F	4 ■	4 ■	1	1½	2	2½	3

▶ *How much yardage do I need for binding?*

Cut/Finished Binding Widths

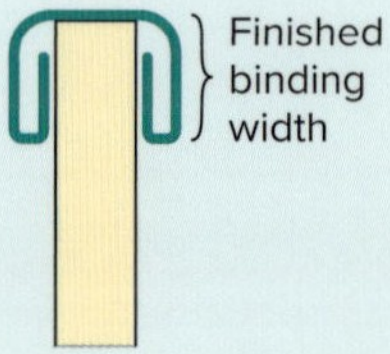

Single-fold binding

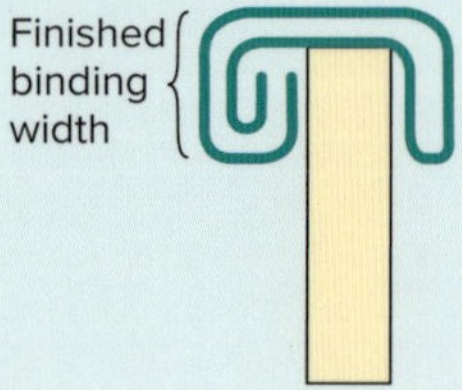

Double-fold binding

FINISHED BINDING WIDTH	1/4″	3/8″	1/2″	3/4″
Double-fold cut width	1 5/8″	2 3/8″	3 1/8″	4 5/8″
Single-fold cut width	1 1/8″	1 5/8″	2 1/8″	3 1/8″

Double-fold width is calculated using (finished width × 6) + 1/8″ extra.

Single-fold width is calculated using (finished width × 4) + 1/8″ extra.

Seam allowance used is the same as the finished binding width.

BONUS BLOCK

Starshine

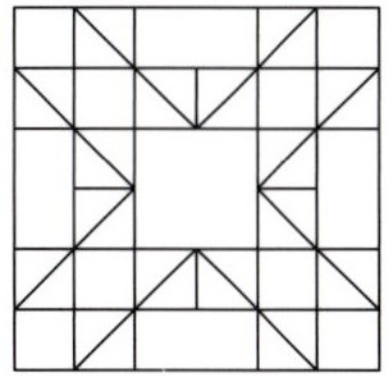

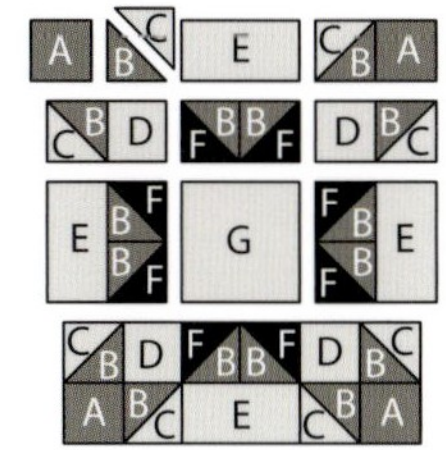

For	Cut	Need	3″	6″	9″	12″	15″
A	4	4	1	1½	2	2½	3
B	8	16	1⅜	1⅞	2⅜	2⅞	3⅜
C	4	8	1⅜	1⅞	2⅜	2⅞	3⅜
D	4	4	1	1½	2	2½	3
E	4	4	1 × 1½	1½ × 2½	2 × 3½	2½ × 4½	3 × 5½
F	4	8	1⅜	1⅞	2⅜	2⅞	3⅜
G	1	1	1½	2½	3½	4½	5½

Yardage for Straight-Grain Binding

PERIMETER of Quilt + 10″ (Inches)	# of Strips	YARDS for 1⅛″-Wide Strips	YARDS for 1½″-Wide Strips	YARDS for 1⅝″-Wide Strips	YARDS for 1¾″-Wide Strips	YARDS for 2⅛″-Wide Strips	YARDS for 2⅜″-Wide Strips	YARDS for 3⅛″-Wide Strips	YARDS for 4⅝″-Wide Strips
80–126	3	⅛	¼	¼	¼	¼	¼	⅓	½
127–168	4	¼	¼	¼	¼	¼	⅓	⅜	⅝
169–210	5	¼	¼	¼	⅓	⅓	⅓	½	⅔
211–252	6	¼	⅓	⅓	⅓	⅜	½	⅝	⅞
253–294	7	¼	⅓	⅓	⅜	½	½	⅝	1
295–336	8	⅓	⅜	⅜	½	½	⅝	¾	1⅛
337–378	9	⅓	½	½	½	⅝	⅝	⅞	1¼
379–420	10	⅓	½	½	½	⅝	¾	1	1⅓
421–462	11	⅜	½	⅝	⅝	¾	⅞	1	1½

Yardage amounts are based on 42″ fabric width. If your fabric is wider or narrower than 42″, make adjustments accordingly.
See the chart on page 33 for cut/finished binding width information for single- and double-fold binding.

BONUS BLOCK

Swamp Angel

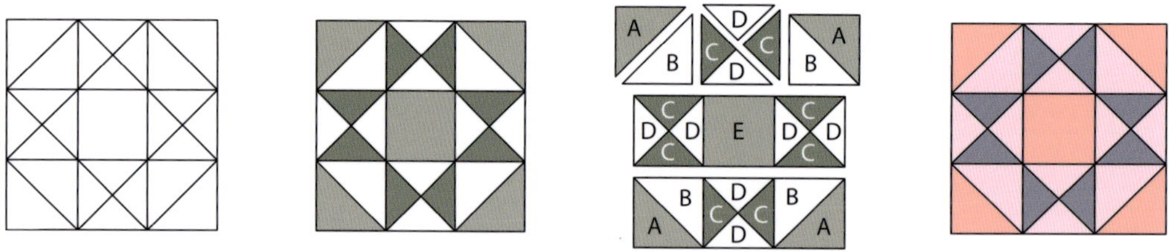

For	Cut	Need	3″	6″	9″	12″	15″
A	2	4	1⅞	2⅞	3⅞	4⅞	5⅞
B	2	4	1⅞	2⅞	3⅞	4⅞	5⅞
C	2	8	2¼	3¼	4¼	5¼	6¼
D	2	8	2¼	3¼	4¼	5¼	6¼
E	1	1	1½	2½	3½	4½	5½

Faux Flange Binding

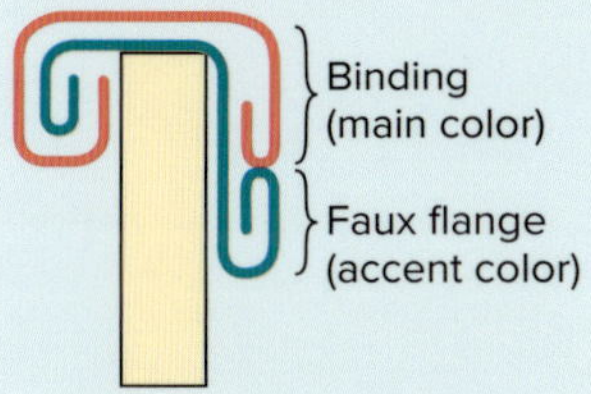

Faux flange binding

Finished binding width	¼″
Finished flange accent width	⅛″
Cut main color binding strips width	1½″
Cut accent strip width	1¾″

Note: It's counterintuitive, but the main binding fabric strip is narrower than the faux flange accent fabric strip.

Faux Flange Binding is a fun and easy way to add a pop of color to your binding by sewing together 2 strips of different fabric to create a narrow "flange" of contrasting color between the quilt top and binding.

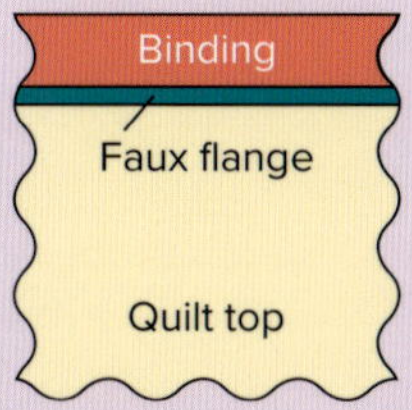

1. See chart on page 34 to determine the number of strips of 1½″ main binding and 1¾″ accent color fabrics.

2. Sew main fabric strips together short end to short end, repeat with the faux flange (accent) fabric strips.

3. Sew main and accent fabrics right sides together along the long edge, press seam open. Fold in half, wrong sides together, press again. (A ⅛″ wide contrasting "faux flange" will be on one side of the binding.)

4. Sew binding to quilt back with "faux flange" side facing quilt back. See instructions for Mitered Double-Fold Binding Corner Construction on page 37 and then bind ends using one of the methods on pages 37–40.

5. To finish, fold binding to quilt front and topstitch "in the ditch" on the seam between the main binding and faux flange accent.

BONUS BLOCK

Tulip Lady Fingers

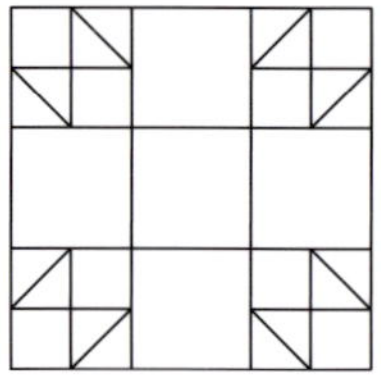

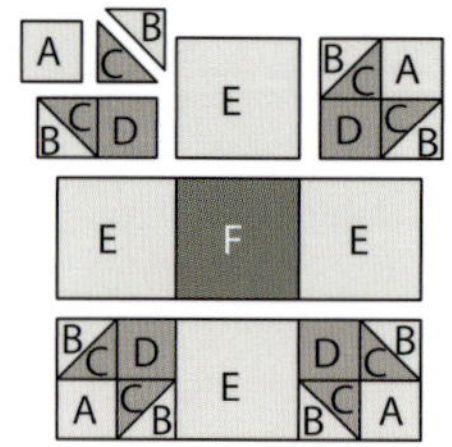

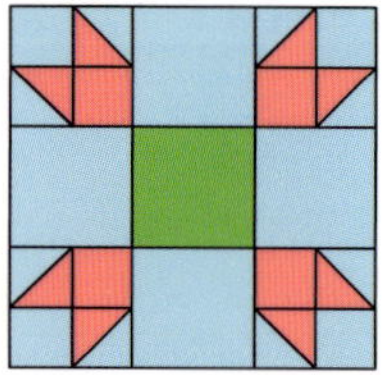

For	Cut	Need	3″	6″	9″	12″	15″
A	4 □	4 □	1	1½	2	2½	3
B	4 □	8 ⧄	1⅜	1⅞	2⅜	2⅞	3⅜
C	4 ■	8 ⧄	1⅜	1⅞	2⅜	2⅞	3⅜
D	4 ■	4 ■	1	1½	2	2½	3
E	4 □	4 □	1½	2½	3½	4½	5½
F	1 ■	1 ■	1½	2½	3½	4½	5½

▶ *How do I cut one long bias strip?*

Cutting Bias Strips

1. Cut the square (see right) in half diagonally and sew the 2 triangles together, using a ¼″ seam.

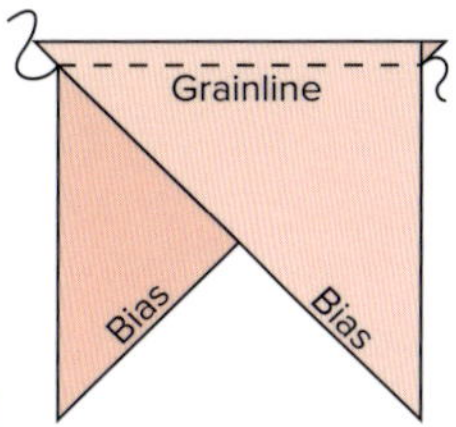

1

2. Press the seam open and mark lines spaced the width you need to cut the bias strips. Cut along the first line about 5″.

2

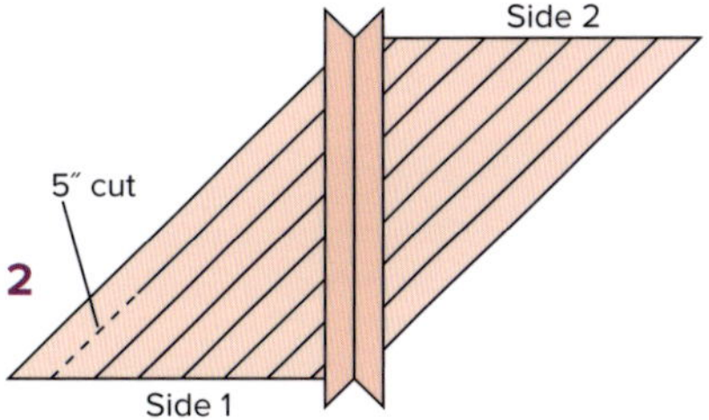

3. Offset by 1 line, pin, and sew into a tube. Continue cutting on the line you started. The tube will become one long bias strip.

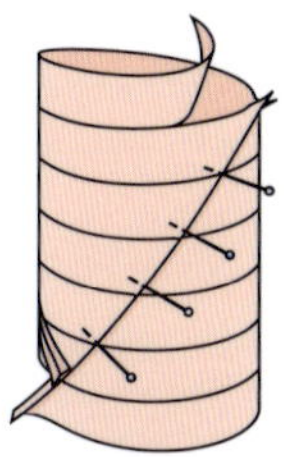

3

Size of the Square Needed for Bias Strips

1st Warning: Prepare yourself but do not be afraid.

2nd Warning: This requires math.

To figure out the size square you'll need to cut bias strips for your quilt, you'll need to do math, and that math includes multiplying by the square root. Don't worry, most people have access to computers or smartphones, and computers and smartphones have access to calculators that can do this for you. (To access the square root function on a smartphone, you may need to select "scientific calculator" vs basic calculator.)

Here's the formula:

Strip width × strip length (in inches) = square inches of area; take the square root of this number + (strip width × 1.414) to find the fabric square size needed.

We recommend adding 16″ to your needed strip length to accommodate seam allowances.

BONUS BLOCK

Union Square B

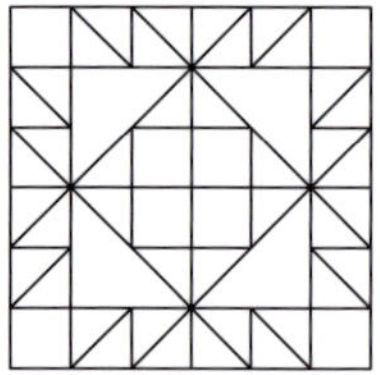

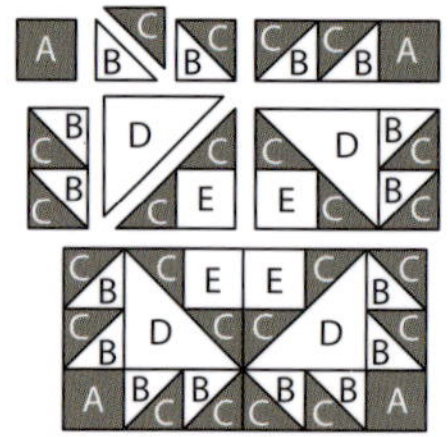

For	Cut	Need	3″	6″	9″	12″	15″
A	4 ■	4 ■	1	1½	2	2½	3
B	8 □	16 ⧄	1⅜	1⅞	2⅜	2⅞	3⅜
C	12 ■	24 ⧄	1⅜	1⅞	2⅜	2⅞	3⅜
D	2 □	4 ⧄	1⅞	2⅞	3⅞	4⅞	5⅞
E	4 □	4 □	1	1½	2	2½	3

How do I miter corners on my binding?

Mitered Double-Fold Binding Corner Construction

1. Join ends of binding strips together with diagonal seams.

2. Fold strips in half lengthwise, wrong sides together, and press. Align raw edges of binding and quilt. Pin. Start stitching 5″ from end of the binding strip. Stop ¼″ from first corner of quilt and backstitch.

3. Turn quilt. Fold binding straight up as shown, forming a 45° fold.

4. Fold binding back down, lining up this second fold with edge of quilt and aligning raw edges. Stitch binding to quilt top, backstitching at each end. Continue for all 4 sides. Stop stitching about 16″ from beginning stitches. See pages 38–40 to seam the binding ends. Wrap binding to other side of quilt, adjust mitered corners, pin, and finish binding using one of the techniques on page 40.

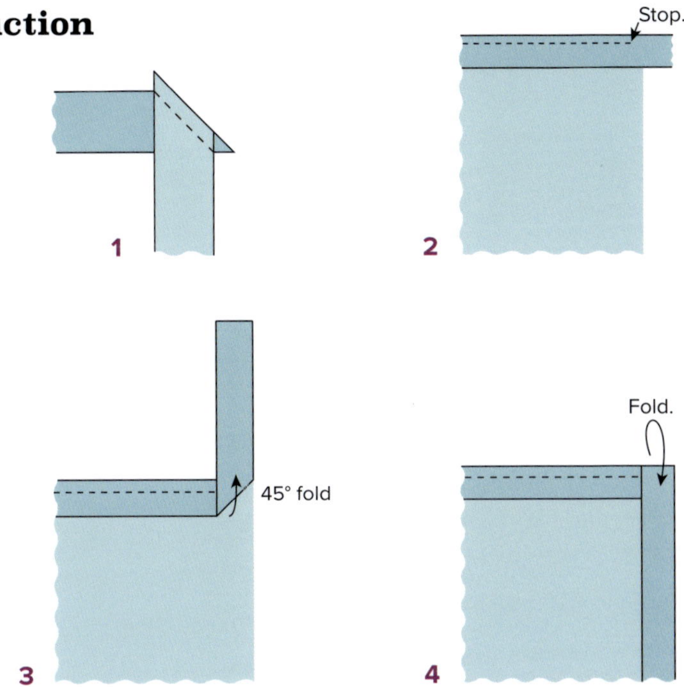

BONUS BLOCK

Variable Star

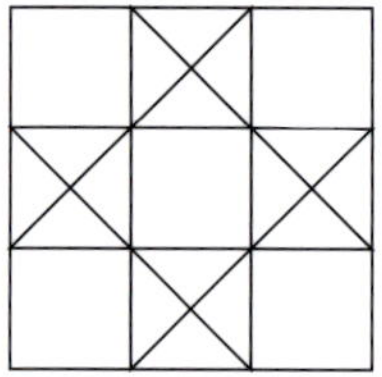

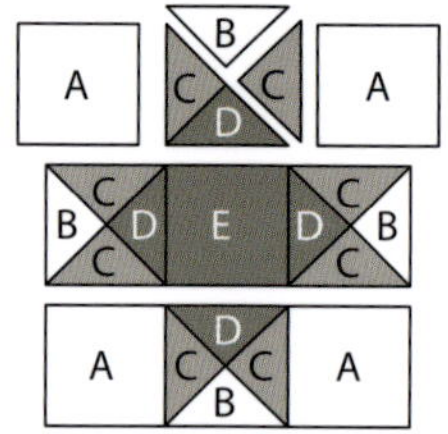

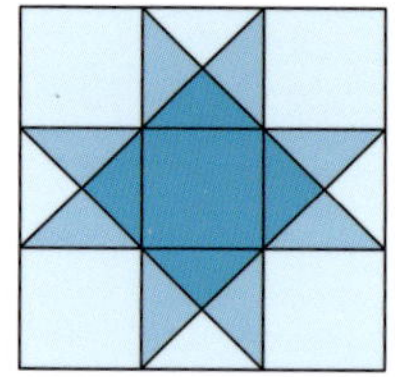

For	Cut	Need	3″	6″	9″	12″	15″
A	4 □	4 □	1½	2½	3½	4½	5½
B	1 □	4 ⊠	2¼	3¼	4¼	5¼	6¼
C	2 ■	8 ⊠	2¼	3¼	4¼	5¼	6¼
D	1 ■	4 ⊠	2¼	3¼	4¼	5¼	6¼
E	1 ■	1 ■	1½	2½	3½	4½	5½

Seaming Double-Fold Binding Ends—Method 1

1. Open End 1 and trim at a 45° angle.

2. Fold and label End 1 as shown.

3. Overlap loose ends of binding where they meet. Lay End 2 binding strip flat. Lay beginning End 1 on top of End 2, keeping both strips folded. Mark Dot A on top layer of End 2. Mark Dot B on bottom layer of End 2.

4. Open End 2 and measure ½″ to the left of dots for seam allowance.

5. Open End 1. With right sides together, stitch End 1 and End 2, using a ¼″ seam allowance. Press seam open, fold joined strip in half, and press. Stitch this binding section in place on quilt.

1

2
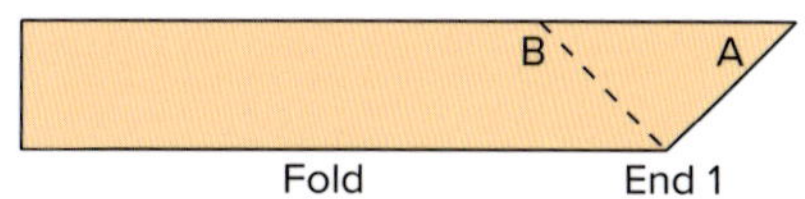

3
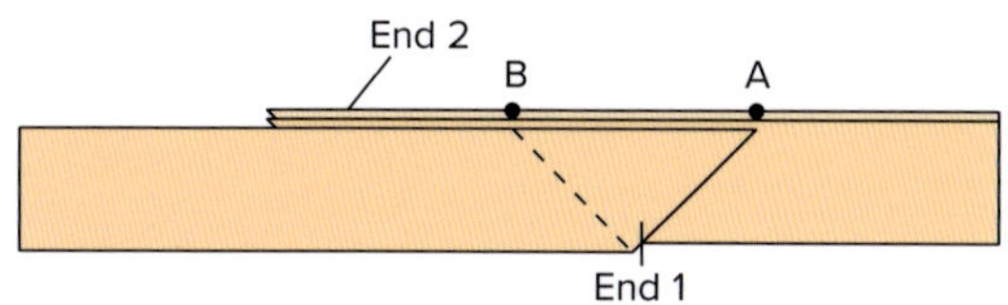

4
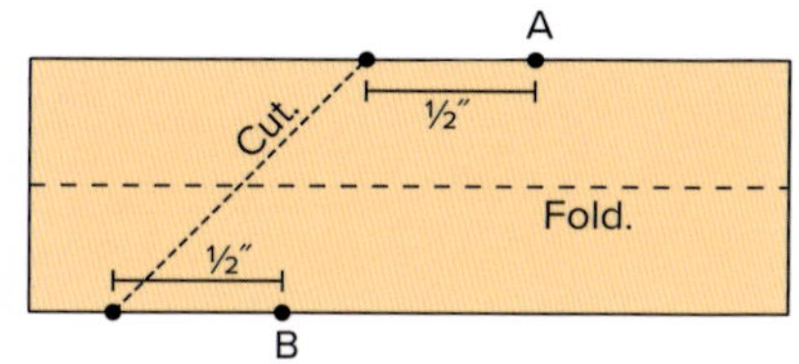

5
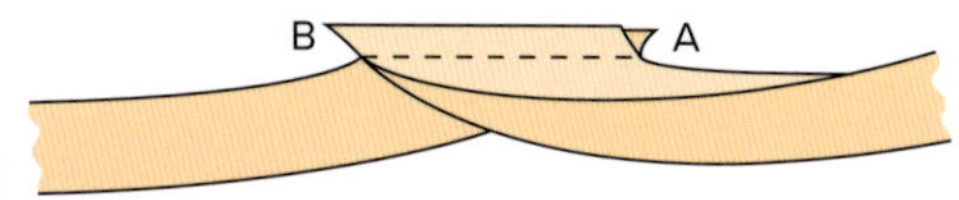

BONUS BLOCK

Walking Star

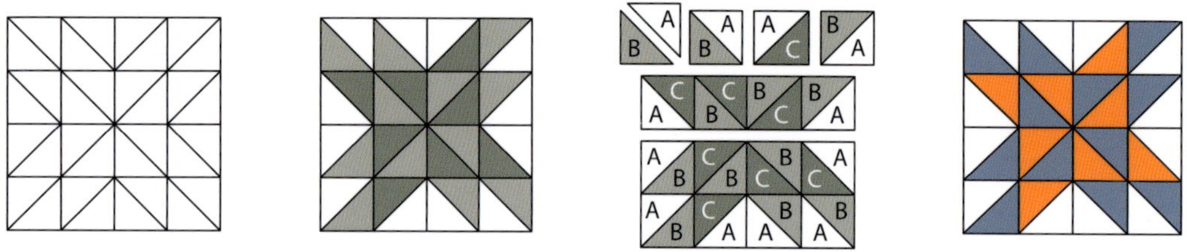

For	Cut	Need	4″	6″	8″	10″	12″
A	6 □	12 ⧄	1⅞	2⅜	2⅞	3⅜	3⅞
B	6 □	12 ⧄	1⅞	2⅜	2⅞	3⅜	3⅞
C	4 □	8 ⧄	1⅞	2⅜	2⅞	3⅜	3⅞

Seaming Double-Fold Binding Ends—Method 2

1. Trim End 1 at a 45° angle. Fold under ¼″ and press.

2. With long fold open, stitch 1 thickness of binding to quilt for about 4″.

3. Lift presser foot and cut threads. Fold binding over to double thickness. Start stitching about ½″ past short edge of point and continue around entire quilt.

4. Lower needle into fabric. Lay end of binding strip over point and single thickness that was the starting point. Cut off End 2 just before stitching that started going through all layers. Tuck end into pocket and finish closing seam.

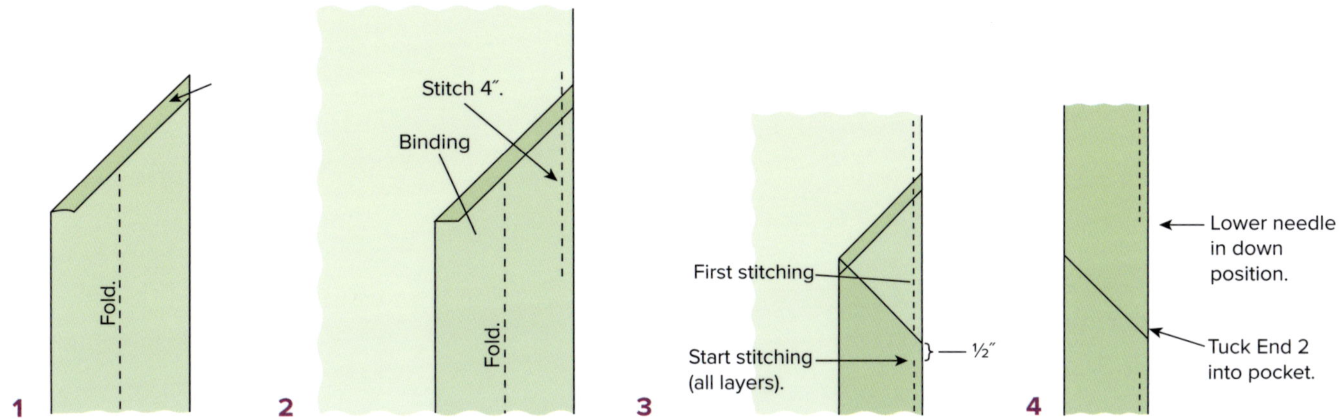

BONUS BLOCK

Water Wheel

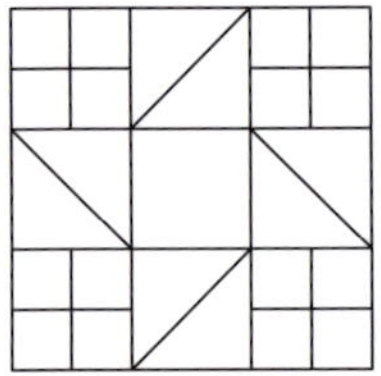

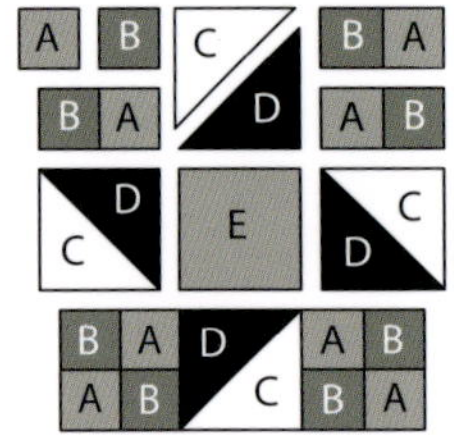

For	Cut	Need	3″	6″	9″	12″	15″
A	8 □	8 □	1	1½	2	2½	3
B	8 ■	8 ■	1	1½	2	2½	3
C	2 □	4 ⧄	1⅞	2⅞	3⅞	4⅞	5⅞
D	2 ■	4 ⧄	1⅞	2⅞	3⅞	4⅞	5⅞
E	1 □	1 □	1½	2½	3½	4½	5½

Seaming Double-Fold Binding Ends—Method 3

1. Fold ending tail of binding back on itself where it meets beginning binding tail. From fold, measure and mark cut width of binding strip. Cut ending binding tail to this measurement. For example, if binding is cut 2⅛″ wide, measure from fold on ending tail of the binding 2⅛″ and cut binding tail to this length.

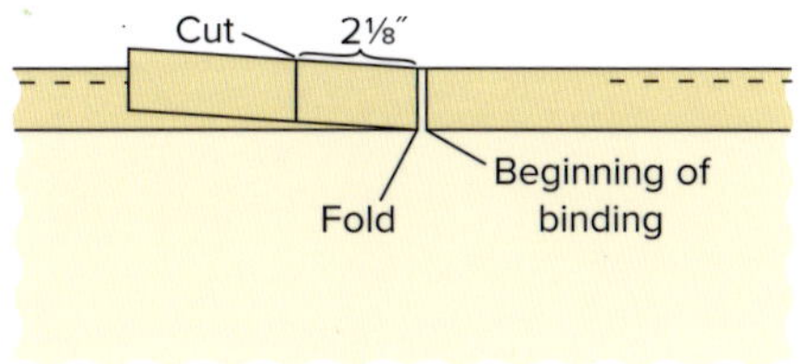

1

2. Open both tails. Place 1 tail on top of the other at right angles, right sides together. Mark diagonal line from corner to corner and stitch on line. Check that you've done it correctly and that binding fits quilt; then trim seam allowance to ¼″. Press open.

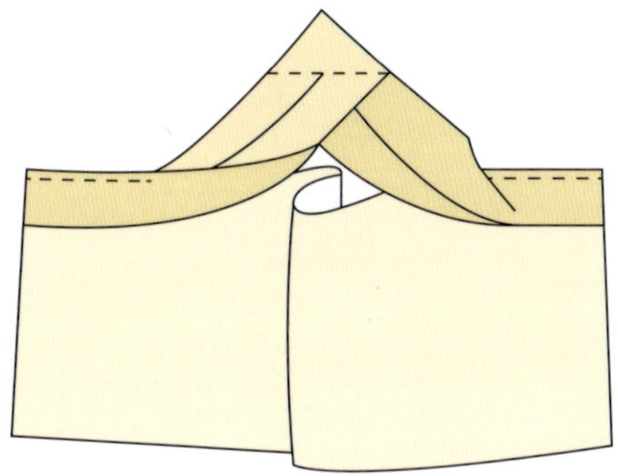
2

3. Refold the binding and stitch this binding section in place on quilt.

Three Options for Finishing Your Binding

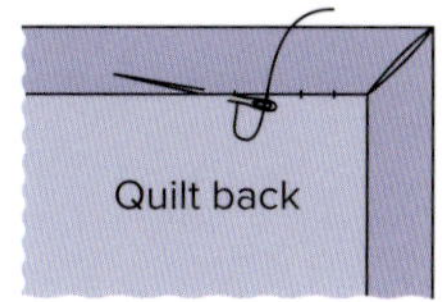

Option 1: Blindstitch binding to back of quilt.

Option 2: Machine straight stitch binding to front of quilt.

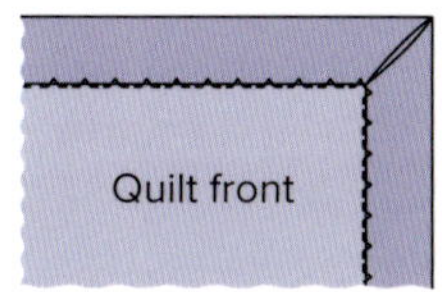

Option 3: Machine blind-hem stitch binding to front of quilt.

Other Great Reference Products
from C&T Publishing

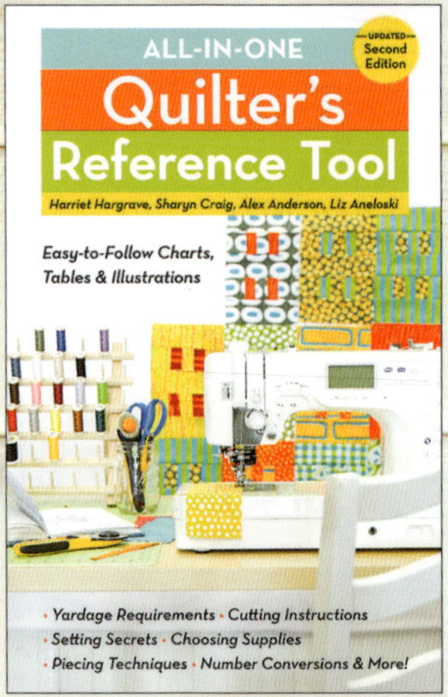

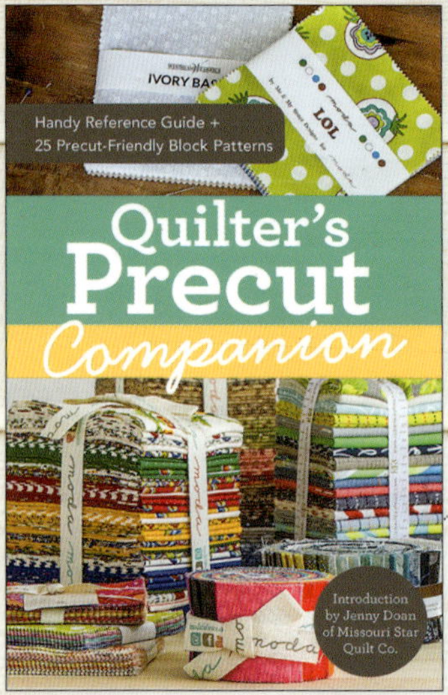